Difference or Disorder?

Understanding Speech and Language Patterns in
Culturally and Linguistically Diverse Students

First Edition

Bilinguistics, Inc.

3636 Executive Center Dr., Suite 268

Austin, TX 78731

Copyright © 2014 Bilinguistics, Inc.

All rights reserved. Printed in the U.S.A.

Published by Bilinguistics, Inc.

3636 Executive Center Dr., Suite 268, Austin, TX 78731

For more information, contact Bilinguistics, Inc. or visit us at: www.bilinguistics.com.

Library of Congress Cataloging-in-Publication Data

ISBN-13: 978-0692254585

ISBN-10: 0692254587

PREFACE

The United States is home to an incredibly diverse population. It is estimated that more than one in five school-age children speak a language other than English at home, and the population of English language learners is projected to continue growing (U.S. Census Bureau, 2008). Given the increasing numbers and diversity of English language learners, it is essential that information about other languages and cultures is easily accessible and applicable for educators. *Difference or Disorder?* provides thorough information that is easily applied to support important decisions about educational placement and services.

The development of this book stemmed from the needs of a group of speech-language pathologists evaluating the speech and language skills of children from many different linguistic and cultural backgrounds. The framework used to distinguish language *differences* from language *disorders* is <u>beneficial for all educators</u>, and the use of this framework will result in improved instructional targets for culturally and linguistically diverse students in the general education classroom, as well as more informed decisions about which students need special education support.

Languages and Dialects

Arabic

Czech

Farsi

French

German

Hebrew

Japanese

Korean

Mandarin

Russian

Spanish

Vietnamese

African-American English

ACKNOWLEDGMENTS

This endeavor is the product of the cumulative efforts of many people. It includes the research of professionals who have studied these languages and dialects, as well as perspectives and input from native speakers of each language. Dr. Ellen Kester started this work nearly a decade ago by comparing and contrasting Spanish and English for use at Bilinguistics and in school districts. When she served as co-chair of the Task Force on Cultural and Linguistic Diversity for the Texas Speech-Language-Hearing Association, she and Margarita Limon-Ordoñez led the Task Force in the development of articles that focused on different languages. Those articles, which received strong praise from the readership of the *Communicologist,* address many languages not addressed in this book and can be accessed on the Texas Speech-Language Hearing Association website.

The Bilinguistics team, which evaluates and works with children from many different language backgrounds each year, carried this work forward. The team is excited and eager to share with other educators. We know it will be a worthwhile resource for all who use it.

Special thanks go to Scott Prath, who oversaw and directed the final production of the project, and Ladaun Jackson, who served as project manager to guide the completion of the chapters. For their efforts in writing, reviewing, and revising these chapters, thanks go to Alisa Baron, Mary Bauman, Alexandra Estrella, Carolyn Artime Gutierrez, Alyson Hendry, Emmy Kolanko, Katherine Marting, Valeritta Liddle, Phuong Lien Palafox, Farinam Pletka, Anna Ubels, Patricia Villarreal, Cristina Villaseñor, and Marie Wirka. The Bilinguistics team also wishes to thank all of the native and near-native speakers whose knowledge and experiences provide personal and cultural perspectives that enrich the information in this book.

CONTENTS

INTRODUCTION

The increasing diversity in the United States has given a new role to educators and speech-language pathologists. Over the past decade, general education teachers have been asked to collect data and track progress on speech and language development for students about whom they have concerns, in order to determine whether or not to refer students for evaluation. Many teachers have expressed uncertainty about how to differentiate speech and language errors that result from native language influences and those that are indicative of speech-language impairment. This same challenge falls on speech-language pathologists, who make diagnostic decisions about students. Many native language influences mimic signs of speech-language impairment, making it impossible to use the same rules for bilingual students that we use for monolingual students. Additionally, the patterns of language influence change depending on the native language of the student, further complicating the decision-making process.

Difference or Disorder? provides educators with information about many different languages. Having identified the most common home languages in the United States (U.S. Census Bureau, 2009), the Bilinguistics team has explored the many linguistic differences of these languages in relation to English. Languages covered by this text include Arabic, Czech, Farsi, French, German, Hebrew, Japanese, Korean, Mandarin, Russian, Spanish, and Vietnamese. There is also a section on African-American English, which is a dialect of American English.

1

Chapter 1
The Framework

Both linguistic and cultural knowledge are critically important when working with families and children from different language backgrounds. Linguistic information, the sound and language systems, and cultural knowledge must be taken into account when determining appropriate educational targets. This information further aids decisions about whether the errors of an English language learner are typical errors or whether those errors are indicative of a language learning disorder. The framework for error analysis provides parents, teachers, and other educators with an effective process for making this distinction. The concept supporting the framework is simple: if sounds or structures exist in both languages, they should not be affected in second language production; if sounds or structures do not exist in both languages, the influence of one language on another can be expected. The goal then is to understand the different sound systems and structures of a language in order to identify which errors are of true concern.

2

Difference or Disorder?

THE SOUND SYSTEMS OF LANGUAGES

When considering the sound systems of two languages, it is necessary to determine which sounds exist in both languages and which sounds are unique to one language or the other. This information helps in the evaluation of speech production errors and aids in determining whether errors could be due to differences in the sound systems of the two languages (Kester & Peña, 2008). Phonotactic constraints, which refer to allowable sound combinations in a particular language (Dell, Reed, Adams, & Meyer, 2000), also are considered. For example, the sounds /np/ cannot occur together at the beginning of a word in English. When considering the information about which phonemes are available in each language and in what patterns or word positions they can occur, it is possible to determine whether errors are expected or not. For example, the unvoiced "th" sound of English does not exist in most dialects of Spanish. Thus, when a Spanish speaker learning English encounters this sound, he or she will most often produce the closest sound that does exist in his or her sound repertoire. For Spanish-speaking bilinguals, in this case, that would be [t].

Linguists have different opinions regarding the phonemic makeup of different languages. For this reason, there are variations in the literature on the consonant and vowel phonemes in each of the languages we have included in *Difference or Disorder?*. Within this text, we have attempted to include all possible phonemes, but have noted when allophonic variations exist. In addition, there are variations in the vowel phonemes included in English, due to dialectal variations. We utilize a set of 12 vowels for the contrastive analyses in this text. The use of Venn diagrams allows for an easy visual representation of sounds that might be problematic for an English language learner across a number of native languages.

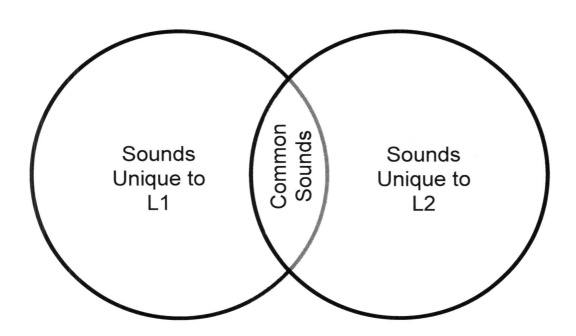

The Venn diagrams present information about the consonants and vowels in English and another language (L1). The diagrams indicate the sounds that are unique to L1, the sounds that are unique to English (L2), and the sounds that are common to both languages. Using this information helps to determine whether errors on certain sounds can be expected. Speech-language evaluators should not be concerned about a child who is only making errors on sounds that are unique to English. However, evaluators should be concerned about a child who is making errors on shared sounds and the unique sounds of his or her native language. That said, evaluators also have to take into account the normal developmental sequence of the sounds. Sounds that are unique to one language or the other also tend to be later occurring sounds.

LANGUAGE STRUCTURES

Aspects of the language systems that help differentiate normal and atypical productions include word order, verb systems, and morphological markers, among other features. When systems or structures differ across languages, English language learners

4

often transfer the structure of their first language to English. For example, adjectives in English are placed in front of nouns (*the blue chair*), whereas adjectives in Spanish follow nouns (*la silla azul*). Thus, an expected error from an English language learner whose native language is Spanish might be, "the chair blue." This book also explores other areas of language structure, such as sentence structure, plurals, past tense, future tense, possessive forms, and much more. The contrastive analyses included in this text focus primarily on differences in the area of form because these differences typically drive the cross-linguistic errors that are encountered in the assessment process.

CULTURAL DIFFERENCES

Culture also plays an important role in understanding language differences versus disorders, especially with respect to pragmatic language skills. Significant variation exists both between and within different cultural groups (Lynch & Hanson, 2004). Exploration of specific cultural patterns can often be misconstrued as stereotyping. In light of this, this text takes a general approach to the discussion of cultural variation by highlighting areas in which cultures may vary rather than emphasizing specific differences between cultures. Chapter 2 provides considerations of different cultural parameters and the possible implications of cultural variation in the educational setting. Further, the Home Corner sections of each chapter are designed to share personal accounts of people from different language backgrounds. These personal accounts serve to increase understanding of the experience of being bilingual and reduce potential bias in understanding the needs and communication patterns of culturally and linguistically diverse learners.

HOW TO USE THIS BOOK

Each individual language chapter contains information about speech sounds, sound patterns, and linguistic structures. All of this information is designed to answer the most common question we all have: *Are the observed speech and language patterns indicative of learning English as a second language or is something more going on?*

Included in each chapter is general information about the language, such as where it is spoken and its prevalence. The language chapters also include norms for speech acquisition when they exist and a contrastive analysis with English speech sounds using Venn diagrams. These diagrams allow readers to literally *see* the differences between the two languages. The same format is used to look at differences in language structure. Developmental norms for language skills are included, as well as the shared and unique features of syntax and morphology in comparison with English. These tables provide a visual clue as to how differences between two languages can result in what appear to be "errors" in English. Finally, in an effort to provide a rich cultural framework in which to consider this information, each chapter includes a personal note from native speakers of the language.

For easy reference, Appendix A features an International Phonetic Alphabet (IPA) chart. Additional developmental information about English sound acquisition, language milestones, and suppression of phonological processes is included in Appendix B in order to facilitate comparison between languages.

REFERENCES

Dell, G. S., Reed, K. D., Adams, D. R., & Meyer, A. S. (2000). Speech errors, phonotactic constraints, and implicit learning: a study of the role of experience in language production. *Journal of Experimental Psychology: Learning, Memory, and Cognition, 26*(6), 1355.

Kester, E. S. & Peña, E. D. (2002). Language ability assessment of Spanish-English bilinguals: Future directions. *Practical Assessment, Research, and Evaluation, 8,* 4.

Lynch, E. W., & Hanson, M. J. (2004). *Developing cross-cultural competence: A guide for working with children and their families* (3rd ed.). Baltimore: Brookes.

Chapter 2
Cultural Considerations

"Multiculturalism is a system of beliefs and behaviors that recognizes and respects the presence of all diverse groups in an organization or society, acknowledges and values their socio-cultural differences, and encourages and enables their continued contribution within an inclusive cultural context which empowers all within the organization or society."

-Caleb Rosado (1996)

Children learn best when they feel accepted and comfortable in their respective environments (Jenson, 2009). As educators, we can foster learning by creating environments in which individual differences are celebrated. The rich culture in the United States can provide challenges for educators, who may need to alter lesson content, teaching approaches, and styles of interaction to successfully impart their knowledge to their students. For many educators, the biggest difficulty lies in knowing when such adjustments are needed. Often information about cultural diversity presents stereotypes that are not appropriately applied to all people within a given cultural group. There is wide variation of cultural norms within a single cultural group. For this reason, this text takes the approach of heightening awareness of cultural variation, rather than focusing on specific cultural differences.

For speech-language pathologists, the American Speech-Language-Hearing Association (ASHA) "acknowledges the need to consider the impact of culture and linguistic exposure/acquisition on all our clients/patients, not simply for minority or diverse clients/patients" (ASHA, 2004). By considering these potential effects of culture, we can ensure the provision of culturally sensitive services. Tomoeda and Bayles (2002) laid out nine cultural parameters for consideration with all children and families. Following their structure, implications for educators are presented for each of their cultural parameters with the goal of increasing understanding in cross-cultural interactions and ultimately improving educational progress and client outcomes (Mahendra et al., 2006).

DESCRIPTIONS OF CULTURAL PARAMETERS

Cultural Parameter	Descriptions	Suggestions
Individualism vs. collectivism	In individualistic cultures, great value is placed on individuals and their rights and decisions; whereas in collectivistic cultures, great value is placed on the group and membership in the group (e.g., extended family).	• Gather information from family members on child's skills and communication environment. • Involve extended family members in decisions on goals and educational planning when appropriate.
Roles of men and women	Gender roles vary across cultures and influence many areas, including education, ownership, choice of profession, and decision-making authority in the family.	Ask the family who participates in educational decisions.

Difference or Disorder?

Cultural Parameter	Descriptions	Suggestions
Views of time and space	Cultures can be schedule-oriented, and adhering to a schedule and punctuality are very important; while others are more event-oriented, and beginning a new event is determined by the completion of the previous event, rather than by a schedule. Different amounts of personal space may be required to feel comfortable.	<ul><li>Explain the importance of arriving on time.</li><li>Encourage early arrival</li><li>Consider effect mode of transportation on arrival time</li><li>Consider adjusting personal space</li><li>Greet with a handshake</li><li>Be prepared for hugs, nods, or bows.</li></ul>
Concepts of class and status	What determines an individual's societal position and place of respect varies across cultures Wealth often plays a large part in the determination of class. Socioeconomic class may result in even greater group dissimilarities than country of origin. If a culture is class conscious, members of different social classes may not socialize together.	<ul><li>Consider sensitivity to social class and status. Address family with formal titles (e.g. "Mr.", "Mrs.", "Dr.") unless asked to use more informal titles.</li></ul>
Values	In some cultures, higher value is placed on self-direction, social traits, and the importance of expressing curiosity; but in other cultures, higher value is placed on conformity, politeness, and obedience.	<ul><li>Ask family what goals are important for them and include them in the child's educational plan.</li><li>Describe the purpose of educational goals for the family.</li><li>Give the family a rationale for selected goals.</li></ul>
Language	In low-context cultures, the actual words are critical and should be the focus of communication. In high-context cultures, nonverbal aspects of communication, such as eye contact, gestures, space, use of silence, and touch are crucial to communicate meaning.	<ul><li>Be aware of your nonverbal communication and what it conveys to the family.</li><li>Observe family interactions.</li><li>Create an environment in which family members feel comfortable expressing their concerns.</li></ul>
Rituals	Weddings, births, deaths, and religious worship are associated with rituals in most cultures.	<ul><li>Consider cultural holidays and celebrations when scheduling sessions.</li><li>Include discussion of holidays and celebrations in lessons.</li></ul>

Cultural Parameter	Descriptions	Suggestions
Beliefs about health	Illness and disabilities are viewed differently across cultures. In some cultures, a person with a disability may be perceived as special, holy, part of God's plan, or out of harmony with nature or the universe. Alternative medicine may be chosen over Western medical practices. Beliefs about health often vary by socioeconomic class.	• Encourage the family to discuss beliefs about health in general, and their child's differences, in particular. • Create an environment in which the family feels comfortable sharing beliefs. • Use questions that are direct but sensitive and non-judgmental. • Explain to parents what "disability" means, keeping in mind the range of implications of such a label.

With regard to the nine cultural considerations above, the main goal for the teacher or clinician is to communicate expectations in a transparent and thoughtful manner. For example, when discussing the start time of the school day, one could say, "School begins at exactly 7:45. We would like for Tony to arrive at 7:30 everyday to have a good start to his day." It is also important to understand that, as educators, we bring our own experiences and customs into each scenario. In turn, when working with those from a culture different from our own, the first step is to disregard judgment and create dialogue and communication when an unexpected scenario takes place. Taking the time to better understand the needs of our families and clients promotes a collaborative relationship that ultimately benefits the student and client.

10

Difference or Disorder?

REFERENCES

American Speech-Language-Hearing Association. (2004). Knowledge and skills needed by speech-language pathologists and audiologists to provide culturally and linguistically appropriate services [Knowledge and Skills]. Available from www.asha.org/policy.

Jenson, E. (2009). *Teaching with poverty in mind.* Alexandria, VA: ASCD.

Mahendra, N., Ribera, J., Sevcik, J. R., Li – Rong, R.A., Cheng, L., McFarland, D. E., Deal – Williams, V. R., Garrett, D., Riquelme, L. F., Salisbury, T., Schneider, W., Villanueva, A. (January 22, 2006). *Why is yogurt good for you? Because it has live cultures.* Retrieved from http://www.asha.org.

Tomoeda, Cheryl K. & Bayles, Kathryn A., (2002, April). *Asha Leader, 7,* p 4-5.

Rosado, C. (1996). *Toward a definition of multiculturalism.* Rosado Consulting.

Chapter 3
Arabic

GENERAL INFORMATION

- **Number of speakers:** More than 200 million speakers worldwide; 11th most-spoken language in the United States

- **Writing system:** Abjad; written from right-to-left; 28 letters

- **Language Family:** Afro-Asiatic, most closely related to Aramaic, Hebrew, Ugaritic and Phoenician; Semitic language

- **Official language in:** Algeria, Bahrain, Chad, Comoros, Djibouti, Egypt, Eritrea, Iraq, Israel, Jordan, Kuwait, Lebanon, Libya, Mauritania, Morocco, Oman, Qatar, Saudi Arabia, Somalia, Sudan, Syria, Tunisia, United Arab Emirates, Yemen

SPECIAL NOTE: "STANDARD" ARABIC

There are more than 30 different varieties of colloquial Arabic, including Egyptian, Algerian, Moroccan/Maghrebi, Sudanese, Saidi, North Levantine, Mesopotamian, and Najdi. Not all dialects are mutually intelligible. Vocabulary and syntactic rules vary among Classic Arabic, Modern Standard Arabic (MSA), and the colloquial dialects. Classic Arabic is used for

Difference or Disorder?

the Qur'an and classic literature. Modern Standard Arabic (MSA) is the universal dialect for all Arabic speakers and is used in formal writing and formal television shows. MSA is not learned as a first language/dialect, but rather as a second language/dialect in school.

This chapter outlines the features of MSA that can serve as a guide to the rules of many dialects. However, when determining whether errors are typical for bilingual development or whether they could be indicative of language impairment, keep in mind that features vary among dialects.

DEVELOPMENTAL NORMS FOR SPEECH

Age	Sounds
1;2-2;0	/b, p, h, m, w, j, d, t, ʔ, š, ʕ, ħ, n, l /
2;0-3;10	/k, q, g, f/
4;0-6;4	/ s, χ, ð, γ, θ, dʒ, s̱, r/
6;5-8;0	/ ṯ, ḏ, ð̱, z/

Note: Underlined consonants are emphatic. Dialectal differences exist.
(Amayreh & Dyson, 1998; 2000; Omar, 1973)

PHONOLOGY AND PHONOTACTICS

Patterns of Native Language Influence:	Example:
Replacement of /p/ with /b/	park – bark
	pig – big
Stops in word-initial position are unaspirated	
Reduction of consonant cluster or addition of /ə/ vowel	play – puhlay
Consonant clusters do not exist in Arabic.	
Replacement of /v/ with /f/	vase – face
Difficulty producing voiced and voiceless "th"	that – dat
	math – mat
Short English vowels that do not occur in	witch – weetch
Arabic may be substituted with a long vowel	sit – seat

Note: Dialectal differences exist and should be considered when referencing the Venn diagrams on the following page. There is high dialectal variation and developmental norms have not been established for many speech sounds.
(Amayreh, 2003; Amayreh & Dyson, 1998; Dyson & Amayreh, 2000)

13

CONTRASTIVE ANALYSIS FOR SPEECH

Venn Contrast: Arabic & English Consonant Phonemes

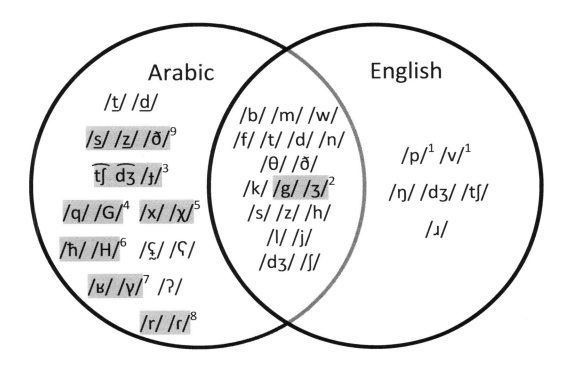

Venn Contrast: Arabic & English Vowel Phonemes

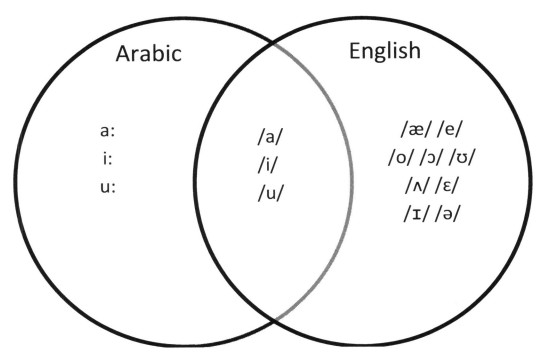

1 Used in borrowed words in some dialects of Arabic. 2-8 Used interchangeably in some dialects of Arabic. 9 Used interchangeably in some dialects but represent distinct phonemes in other dialects. Underlined phonemes are emphatic and are produced with secondary pharyngeal articulation. (Amayreh, 2003; Amayreh & Dyson, 1998; Arabic Language, 2013; Dyson & Amayreh, 2007)

CONTRASTIVE ANALYSIS OF LANGUAGE: MORPHOSYNTAX

Note: Sentences marked with an asterisk (*) are not grammatical.

Feature	Arabic	English	Examples of Errors
Word order	Subject-Verb-Object (MSA & many colloquial Arabic dialects)	Strict Subject-Verb-Object order	He went Brian to the school.* /Brian went to school.
Possessives	Possessor follows object.	____'s (singular noun) ____s' (plural noun)	This is the book the teacher. * /This is the teacher's book.
Adjectives	Adjective follows noun	Adjective precedes noun	The ball big. */ The big ball.
Verb inflection	10 verbal forms: Each set has its own set of active and passive participles Imperfect and perfect aspect forms of each verb also exist.	2 present tense forms: I eat You eat He eats We eat You all eat They eat Past tense uses the same form for each person.	A variety of verb errors, including unmarked third person present: He walk to the store. * /He walks to the store.
Modal verbs	Do not exist	Do exist	From the possible that I am late. * /I may be late.
Definite articles	The definite article "al" is a prefix attached to a noun	Definite articles are words that precede the noun	Alcoffee is ready.*/The coffee is ready.
Indefinite articles	Do not exist	Do exist	I gave him sheet of paper. * /I gave him a sheet of paper.
Question formation	Questions are marked by a question word; no change in word order	Word order inversion or addition of "do"	When I can call you? * /When can I call you?
Nominal sentence	One of the most common sentence structures	Less common; typically used in rhetoric or casual speech	I boy.*/I am a boy.

15

Feature	Arabic	English	Examples of Errors
Prepositions	Exist but there is not a one-to-one correspondence with English prepositions. *Some prepositions in English do not exist in colloquial Arabic	Exist but there is not a one-to-one correspondence with Arabic prepositions	Preposition substitution or redundancy: Go in inside the house. * /Go inside the house. I picked up your umbrella for mistake. * /I picked up your umbrella by mistake.
Auxillary verbs	Do not exist	Exist	Deletion of has/have in present perfect tense and auxiliary redundancy: They are will be resting. * /They were resting.
Present tense verb 'to be'	Does not exist	Exists	I working tomorrow. */I am working tomorrow.

(Ager, 2013; Anbray, 2011; Lewis, Simons, & Fennig, 2013; Noor, 1996; Shoebottom, 2012; Thompson, 2013)

SPECIAL NOTE: VOCABULARY ERRORS

A common mistake made by Arabic speakers acquiring English is the use of "he" for "she" because "he" sounds similar to the Arabic word meaning "she." Also, Arabic speakers may use "who" for "he" because "who" sounds very similar to the Arabic word for "he."

HOME CORNER

I grew up in Lebanon, a country where English, Arabic, and French are pretty much interchangeable. At home, I predominantly spoke Arabic. At school, I predominantly spoke French, but in college I mostly spoke English.

Language was never anything I thought about and I definitely took it for granted. I was even disappointed in myself because I thought I didn't know how to speak "another" language. It wasn't until I moved to the United States that I started realizing how lucky I was to speak three languages so fluently and effortlessly. I did, however, notice a major change

Difference or Disorder?

in how I spoke those languages. In Lebanon, while I would predominantly speak one language, I was always switching back and forth, aiding myself with the other two when they better expressed what I was trying to say. After moving the U.S., I found myself speaking only English for the first time in my life. While it wasn't exactly difficult, it was a noticeable change and nowadays, after being in America for almost five years, I find that English has become my strongest language and the only one I use when I am expressing myself beyond daily conversations.

Nai Obeid, Artist

FUN FACT: In Persia, the official language was Parsi, which is more commonly known today as Farsi. Why? Because when the Arabs at one point took over the area, they did not have the /p/ sound in their phonetic inventory, so they substituted /f/.

REFERENCES

Ager, S. (2013, October 24). *Arabic.* Retrieved from
      http://www.omniglot.com/writing/arabic.htm

Amayreh, M. M. (2003). Completion of consonant inventory of Arabic. *Journal of Speech, Language, and Hearing Research, 46,* 3, 517-529.

Amayreh, M.M., & Dyson, A. (1998). *The acquisition of Arabic consonants.* Journal of Speech, Language, and Hearing Research, 41, 642-653.

Amayreh, M M., & Dyson, A. T. (2000). Phonetic inventories of young Arabic-speaking children. *Clinical Linguistics and Phonetics, 14,* 3, 193-215.

Anbray. (2011, November 27). *Understanding the errors of Arabic speaking ELL's.* [Slideshare presentation]. Retrieved from http://www.slideshare.net/anbray723/understanding-the-errors-of-arabic-speaking-ells

Arabic language. (n.d.). Retrieved October 24, 2013 from Wikipedia Online: http://en.wikipedia.org/wiki/Arabic_language

Dyson, A. T., & Amayreh, M. M. (2000). Phonological errors and sound changes in Arabic-speaking children. *Clinical Linguistics and Phonetics, 14,* 79-109.

Dyson, A. T., & Amayreh, M. M. (2007). Jordanian Arabic Speech Acquisition. In S. McLeod (ed.). *The International Guide to Speech Acquisition,* Clifton Park, NY: Thomson Delmar Learning.

Learn Arabic. (2013, October 24). Retrieved from http://arabic.speak7.com/arabic_pronouns.htm

Lewis, M., Simons, G., & Fennig, C. (2013) *Ethnologue: Languages of the world, Seventeenth edition.* Retrieved from http://www.ethnologue.com

Noor, H. H. (1996). *English Syntactic Errors by Arabic Speaking Learners: Reviewed.*

Omar, M. K. (1973). The acquisition of Egyptian Arabic as a native language. *Janva linguarum: Series practica, 160*, 199-205.

Shoebottom, P. (2012, February 24). *The differences between English and Arabic.* Retrieved from http://esl.fis.edu/grammar/langdiff/arabic.htm

Thompson, I., (2013, April 10). *Arabic (Modern standard).* Retrieved from http://aboutworldlanguages.com/arabic-modern-standard

18

Chapter 4
Czech

GENERAL INFORMATION

- **Number of speakers:** 9.2 million speakers in Czech Republic and 9.5 million worldwide

- **Writing system:** Latin alphabet with diacritic marks above some letters that indicate longer or softer sounds. There are three different diacritical marks. There is a one-to-one correspondence between letters and sounds.

- **Language Family:** Indo-European–Slavic—West—Czech-Slovak

- **Official language in:** Czech Republic

PHONOLOGY AND PHONOTACTICS

Patterns of Native Language Influence:	Example:
Replacement of voiceless "th" (θ) with /t/	thumb – tum
Replacement of voiced "th" (ð) with /d/ or /z/	they – dey OR zey
Replacement of /w/ with /v/	what – vat
	why – vy
/ɹ/ distorted in all positions, often resembling a trilled /r/ in initial position	rabbit - rrrabbit
Voiced consonants (i.e. /d/, /v/) are devoiced in the final position of words	dog – dok
	five – fife

CONTRASTIVE ANALYSIS FOR SPEECH

Venn Contrast: Czech & English Consonant Phonemes

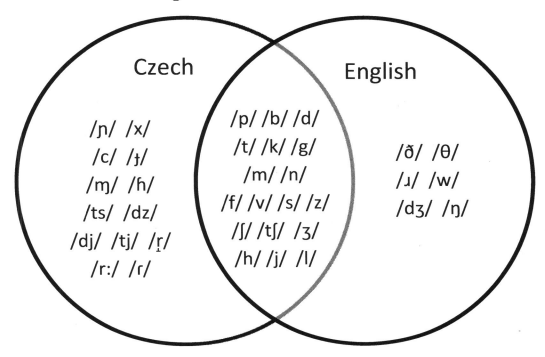

Venn Contrast: Czech & English Vowel Phonemes

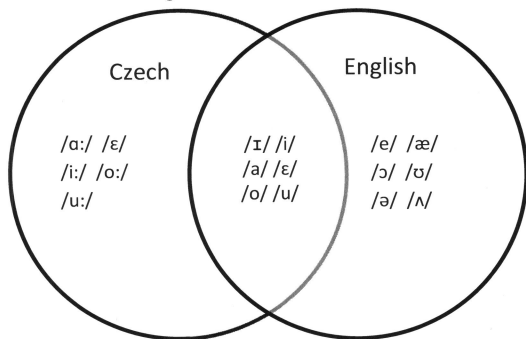

(Czech, n.d.; Czech Phonology, n.d.; IPA for Czech and Slovak, n.d.; Native Phonetic Inventory, n.d.)

Difference or Disorder?

CONTRASTIVE ANALYSIS OF LANGUAGE: MORPHOSYNTAX

Note: Sentences marked with an asterisk (*) are not grammatical.

Feature	Czech	English	Examples of Errors
Word order	Flexible. Allowed orders include: SVO, OVS, SOV, OSV.	Strict Subject-Verb-Object order	To store went by car aunt.* /My aunt went to the store.
Possessives	Add different ending to name or object that is possessed	's	The dog of my mother is sick.*/My mother's dog is sick.
Verb inflection	5-6 forms, determined by subject: Ja (I) Jím Ty (you-informal) Jíš Vy (you-formal) Jíte On, Ona, Ono(He, she, it) Jí My (we) Jíme Oní (they) Její	2 present tense forms: I eat You eat He/She/It eats We eat They eat	A variety of verb errors. Unmarked third person present tense is a common error. He eat bread.*/He eats bread.
Pronouns	Pronouns are omitted when they can be inferred from context.	Pronoun is always required	Drinks water.*/He drinks water.
Regular past tense	Many forms, determined by subject	One form (-ed)	Past tense verbs may be unmarked: He play baseball.*/ He played baseball.
Negatives	"no" precedes verb	"not" follows copula, "don't/doesn't" precedes any other verb	She not eat. */ She doesn't eat.
Double negatives	Allowed	Not allowed	I don't want no more. */ I don't want any more.
Question formation	Marked by inflection	Word order inversion or addition of "do"	You like this?*/ Do you like this?
Articles	Do not exist	One definite: *the*; two indefinite: *a, an*	I have dog.*/ I have a dog.
Prepositions	Present, but there is not a 1:1 correspondence with English prepositions	Present, but there is not a one-to-one correspondence with Czech prepositions.	I saw it in television.*/ I saw it on television.
Present continuous verb form	Does not exist	Exists	I drink a soda now.*/ I'm drinking a soda now.

(Barton, 2012; Czech, n.d.; Remediosova & Cechova, 2005)

21

HOME CORNER

I moved to the United States from Prague, Czech Republic at 17, so I didn't have the experience of growing up in a community different than my own. I did not know any English when I arrived so it was difficult to make friends in the beginning. I moved to a small rural area of Tennessee and felt separated from other kids my age because of the language barrier. I think the hardest part was that I liked to make jokes, but not understanding the language or culture well enough, I was unable to show my funny side. Instead of going out, I stayed home and watched tons of American movies, mostly comedies. That was how my English grew, and I learned jokes that were relevant to American culture.

After high school, I went to college in Arkansas where I was able to make lots of close friends. It became much easier to have conversations and joke with them. I was finally able to show my personality in English, and it helped me make connections with new people and form long-time friendships.

Ivo Pletka, Graduate student

REFERENCES

Barton, M. (2012). 20 Common English Mistakes Made by Czech People. Retrieved February 10, 2014, from English Current: http://www.englishcurrent.com/esl-materials-2/common-english-mistakes-czech-people/

Czech (n.d.). In *Ethnologue.* Retrieved August 10, 2013, from http://www.ethnologue.com/language/ces

Czech Phonology (n.d.) . In *Wikipedia.* Retrieved February 10, 2014, from http://en.wikipedia.org/wiki/Czech_phonology

IPA for Czech and Slovak (n.d.) In *Wikipedia.* Retrieved Octover 17, 2014 from http://en.wikipedia.org/wiki/Help:IPA_for_Czech_and_Slovak

Native Phonetic Inventory: Czech (n.d.). In *The Speech Accent Archive.* Retrieved Octover 27, 2014.

Remediosova, H., & Cechova, E. (2005). Do You Want to Speak Czech? Czech Republic: Liberec.

Chapter 5
Farsi

"Stay close to any sounds that make you glad that you are alive."

-Hafiz (14th century)

GENERAL INFORMATION

- **Number of speakers:** More than 56 million speakers worldwide. 140,695 Persian speakers in U.S. (Farsi, Dari, Iranian, Tajik) (U.S. Census Bureau, 2011).

- **Writing system:** Includes but not limited to Arabic script with 32 letters (compared to 28 Arabic letters). Written from right to left.

- **Language Family:** Indo—European—Indo-Iranian—Iranian—Western—Southwestern—Persian

- **Official language in**: Iran (Persian) and Afghanistan (Dari)

CONTRASTIVE ANALYSIS FOR SPEECH

Venn Contrast: Farsi & English Consonant Phonemes

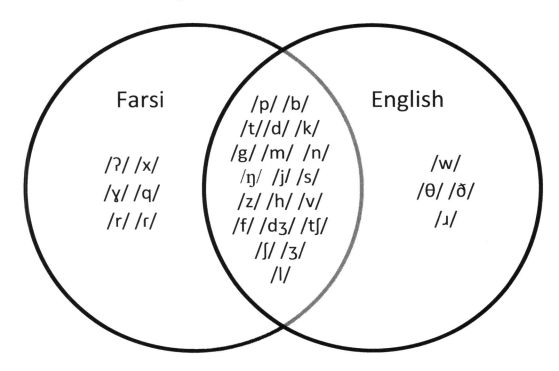

Venn Contrast: Farsi & English Vowel Phonemes

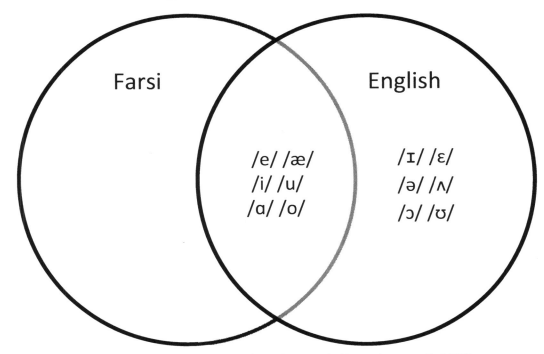

(Hall, 2007; IPA for Persian, n.d.; Lewis, 2014; Persian Phonology, n.d.; Yarmohammedi, 1996)

Difference or Disorder?

PHONOLOGY AND PHONOTACTICS

Patterns of Native Language Influence:	Example:
Replacement of voiceless "th" (θ) with /t/ or /s/	thumb – tum mouth – mous
Replacement of voiced "th" (ð) with /d/ or /z/ in all positions	they – dey these – zeese
Addition of /ɛ/ in front of /st/ clusters	stop-estop store-estore
In Farsi, words cannot start with an clusters beginning with /s/.	
Replacement of /w/ with /v/	what-vat why-vy
Distortion of /ɹ/ in all positions, often resembling a trilled /r/ in initial position	/ɾ/ may be distorted in a variety of ways
Short English vowels that do not occur in Farsi may be substituted with a long vowel equivalent	witch – weetch ditch-deetch

CONTRASTIVE ANALYSIS OF LANGUAGE: MORPHOSYNTAX

Note: Sentences marked with an asterisk (*) are not grammatical.

Feature	Farsi	English	Examples of Errors
Word order	Flexible	Strict Subject-Verb-Object	Ali pen took. */Ali took the pen.
Pronoun gender	One word for third person singular	Three words for third person singular (he, she, it)	(when talking about a boy) She drinks water*/He drinks water.
Adjectives	Adjective follows noun	Adjective precedes noun	The ball big*/ The big ball.
Use of subject pronouns	Pro-drop: pronoun is not required	Pronoun is always required	Drinks water*/He drinks water.
Articles	No articles	Articles present before nouns	I went to store*/I went to the store.
Preposition marking direction	Does not exist	"to"	I go school*/I go to school.
Question formation	Questions marked by inflection	Word order inversion or addition of "do"	You give me water?*/ Will you give me a water?

25

Feature	Farsi	English	Examples of Errors
Verb inflection	6-7 forms, determined by subject: Mæn (I) meekhoram To (you-informal)/Shomah (you-formal) meekhoree/Shom ah (you-formal/plural) meekhoreen/mee khoreed Oo (He, she, it) meekhoreh Ma (We) meekhoreem Oona/Anha/Ishan (they) meekhoran	2 present tense forms: I eat You eat He eats We eat You all eat They eat	She talk to me.* / She talks to me.
Regular past tense	5-6 forms, determined by subject	One form for all subjects	The simplest form is often used. She walk to the store* /She walked to the store.

(Farsi & Zared, 2013; Mobaraki, 2007; Yarmohammedi, 1996)

HOME CORNER

Born in Arizona, I moved at a very young age to the small town of Jonesboro, Arkansas. My sisters and I were first-generation Americans, and my parents had not yet received their citizenship. It was the early 90's when we arrived, and we stood out. Our dark features were a great contrast to the average person living in this town with a population of 50,000. I learned early on, by the negative reactions people would have when it came out that I was Iranian, that it was best to just say I was Persian. To be Iranian associated me with the negative stereotypes associated with the broken relationship between Iran and the U.S. To be Persian didn't mean much of anything to people. In fact, many people assumed it meant I was from Paris.

Difference or Disorder?

My parents naturally had an accent, which frequently embarrassed me because it "gave us away" and there was always a breakdown in communication (especially with the strong southern drawl). I always felt self-conscious when people would ask about my heritage and culture because I sensed that the questions came from a place of judgment and pre-conceived ideas of what it meant to be Iranian. Frequently, I would be asked where my name is from and when I would say "Iran," more often than not, I would get a blank look and a simple, "Oh," as a response.

Luckily, I had a few friends that thought it was neat that I could speak another language and wished they could talk in "code" when in public. I never really thought it special or cool to speak another language, but I did find it very useful when I didn't want someone to understand what I was saying.

As I grew up and became a young adult, the town slowly grew and became more diverse. This didn't necessarily change people's point of view, but I was able to meet more people who were like me, (i.e., from a different culture or who spoke a different language).

Now I have found myself very lucky to be Iranian and to speak Farsi. It has helped me professionally to serve children and their families who speak Farsi as well as allowed me to connect with a wide array of people who share a similar cultural background.

Farinam Pletka, Bilingual Speech-Language Pathologist

REFERENCES

Farsi, M., & Zarel, L. (2013). Practical contrastive analysis of English and Persian with special emphasis on relative clauses. *The Journal of Arts and Educational Research*, 7-9.

Hall, M. (2007). Phonological Characteristics of Farsi Speakers Of English and L1 Australian English. *Speakers' Perceptions Of Proficiency*. Retrieved Octover 17, 2014 from http://www.asian-efl-journal.com/Thesis-M-Hall.pdf

IPA for Persian (n.d.). In Wikipedia. Retrieved Octover 17, 2014 from
http://en.wikipedia.org/wiki/Help:IPA_for_Persian

Lewis, M. P. (2014). Ethnologue. *Languages of the World, Seventeenth Edition.*
Gary F. Simons, & Charles D. Fennig (eds.). Dallas, TX: SIL International.
Online version: http://www.ethnologue.com

Mobaraki, Mohsen (2007). Functional categories in the L2 acquisition of English
morpho-syntax: a longitudinal study of two Farsi-speaking children. Doctoral
theses, Durham University. Available at Durham E-Theses Online:
http://etheses.dur.ac.uk/2568/

Persian phonology (n.d.). In *Wikipedia.* Retrieved February 13, 2014, from
http://en.wikipedia.org/wiki/Farsi_phonology.

U.S. Census Bureau (2011). American Community Survey.

Yarmohammedi, L. (1996). *A contrastive analysis of Persian and English.* Payame
Noor University Press.

Chapter 6
French

GENERAL INFORMATION

- **Number of speakers:** More than 68 million speakers worldwide; 2.07 million speakers above the age of 5 in the United States (U.S. Census, 2010)

- **Writing system:** Latin script

- **Language Family:** Indo-European—Italic—Romance

- **Official language in:** France, Democratic Republic of the Congo, Canada, Madagascar, Cameroon, Ivory Coast, Burkina Faso, Niger, Senegal, Mali, Rwanda, Belgium, Guinea, Chad, Haiti, Burundi, Benin, Switzerland, Togo, Central African Republic, Republic of the Congo, Gabon, Comoros, Equatorial Guinea, Djibouti, Luxembourg, Vanuatu, Seychelles, and Monaco.

DEVELOPMENTAL NORMS FOR SPEECH

Age	Sounds
<36 months	/p, t, m, n, f, z, ɲ/
36-53 months	/b, d, k, g, v, l, w, ʁ, ɥ/
53+ months	/s, j, ʃ, ʒ/

(Rvachew et al., 2013)

CONTRASTIVE ANALYSIS FOR SPEECH

Venn Contrast: French & English Consonant Phonemes

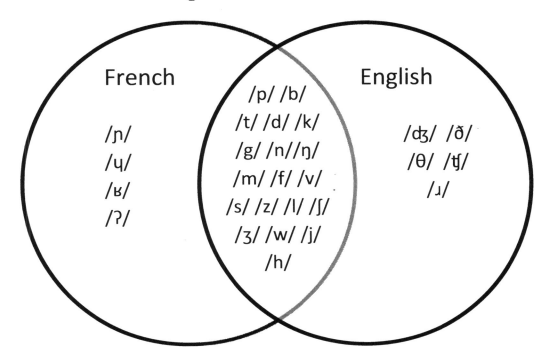

Venn Contrast: French & English Vowel Phonemes

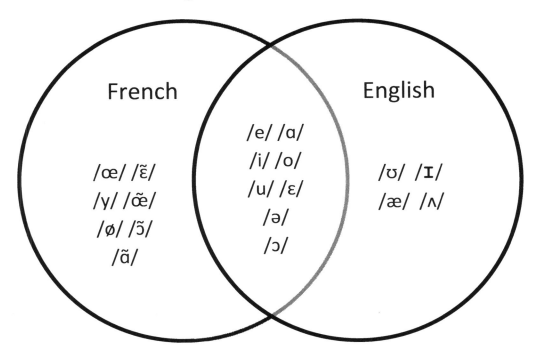

Note: The consonants and vowels included in these Venn diagrams represent the Parisian dialect of French. Other dialects vary. Some dialects include /r/ and /ɾ/.

(Brousseau-Lapré & Rvachew, 2014; David & Wei, 2008; IPA for French, n.d.)

Difference or Disorder?

PHONOLOGY AND PHONOTACTICS

Patterns of Native Language Influence:	Example:
Replacement of voiceless "th" (θ) with /s/ or /t/ in all positions	thumb – sum OR tum mouth – mous OR mout
Replacement of voiced "th" (ð) with /z/ or /d/ in all positions	they – zey OR dey other – ozer OR oder
Omission of /h/ in all positions	how – 'ow happy – 'appy
Replacement of "ch" with "sh" in all positions	chocolate – shocolate chicken – shicken
Omission of /z/ allophone of plural /s/	dogs - dog
/ɹ/ distortion or deletion	father – fatha
Overproduction of /ɪ/ and –ing	going – /goɪŋgə/ ("going-guh") smile – /smaɪlə/ ("smile-luh")
These sounds are softer and often unreleased in English. French speakers may overemphasize them and sometimes add a schwa /ə/ sound after them.	
All syllables of equal length, no reduction of unstressed vowels to schwa /ə/	DIFficulty (/dɪfəkəltɨ/) - DIFFICULTY (/difikulti/)
English is known as a stress-timed language and French is known as a syllable-timed language. In English, unstressed syllables are noticeably shorter than stressed ones and the vowel is usually reduced to a schwa..	*Note:* A French speaker may not adequately shorten unstressed syllables in a multisyllabic word or may produce the vowel the same in every word regardless of stress.
Replacement of /ɪ/ with /i/	witch – weetch
Short English vowels that do not occur in French may be substituted with a long vowel equivalent.	
Replacement of /e/ with /ɛ/	wait - wet
Tense or long English vowels that do not occur in French may be substituted with a lax or short vowel equivalent.	
Stops in word-initial position are unaspirated	/pʰig/ - /pig/ (will sound more like "big")
Nasalization of vowels	dance – /dãs/ instead of /dænts/
French has four nasal vowels (/ɛ̃/ /œ̃/ /ɔ̃/ /ɑ̃/), which are represented in written words by one or more vowels followed by a single /n/ ("-ain", "-in", "-un", "-en", etc.) These vowels do not exist in English.	

(Brosseau-Lapré & Rvachew, 2013; Lefebvre et al., 2008; Maillart et al., 2004; Maillart & Parisse, 2008)

CONTRASTIVE ANALYSIS FOR LANGUAGE: MORPHOSYNTAX

Note: Sentences marked with an asterisk (*) are not grammatical.

Feature	French	English	Examples of Errors
Possessives	De _____	_____'s (singular nouns) _____s' (plural nouns)	The car of my mom is broken.*/ My mom's car is broken.
Adjectives	Adjective follows noun (usually, though there are exceptions)	Adjective precedes noun	The test difficult starts at 3.*/ The difficult test starts at 3.
Regular past tense verb inflection	5-6 forms, determined by subject J'ai marché – I walked Tu as marché – You walked Il/Elle a marché – He/She walked Nous avons marché – We walked Vous avez marché – You (plural) walked Ils/Elles avont marché – They walked	One form for all subjects	She walk to the store* / She walked to the store.
Irregular past tense	Irregular verbs do not correspond to those in English	Irregular verbs do not correspond to those in French	I eat a hamburger*/I ate a hamburger.
Multi-purpose verbs	Verbs with multiple meanings that do not correspond across languages	Verbs with multiple meanings that do not correspond across languages	I have four years*/ I am four years old. Do you have hunger?*/ Are you hungry?
Present progressive verb tense	Expressed by using the present tense verb form	Add –ing to verb	I read the book now.*/I'm reading the book now.
Question formation	Questions marked by word order inversion, inflection, or additions of est-ce que	Word order inversion or addition of do	What means this word?*/ What does this word mean? What you think?*/ What do you think? We can go?* / Can we go?

(Boudreault et al., 2007; David & Wei, 2008; Desmarais et al, 2010; Kayne, 1981; MacLeod et al., 2014; Royle & Valois, 2010; Sylvestre et al., 2012; ; Thordardottir, 2005; Thordardottir et al., 2010)

Difference or Disorder?

HOME CORNER

When I moved to Paris in 2009, my goal was to speak French as if it were my native language. I remember listening attentively to the ways people around me pronounced the sounds that my brain was not used to hearing and trying to repeat these sounds as naturally as possible. For the first few years, upon hearing me speak French for the first time, people consistently asked me where I was from. Although this gave me an opportunity to speak about my country and my culture, it always reminded me that I was not fully integrated and, from my point of view, not fully accepted. I wanted people to know me as "Cole," not "Cole the American," and this meant that I must speak French as naturally as I speak English. I had to stop thinking in English, stop reading in English, stop listening to music in English and, above all, avoid speaking English (other than over the phone with my friends and family in the United States). I also had to avoid all American communities and make as many contacts in France as possible. To some people, it was as if I had rejected my own culture, but for me, it was the opportunity of a lifetime to develop a double culture.

Being a true part of France was, and still is, a necessity for me. Over the past few years, I have had many opportunities to experience France as if I were a native. I have worked as an English teacher in three French elementary schools and as an educational assistant in two French high schools. I earned a master's degree from a French business school and was hired to work for a French company near the beautiful Champs-Élysées Avenue in Paris. It isn't a question of intelligence or capability, but one of passion and desire to become a part of a culture that I have adopted as my own. Today, when I meet people for the first time, they ask me what I do for a living, what I do in my free time, etc. And only when they ask me where I am from do they discover my American origins. I am very proud to be American and to share my culture and my point of view as I continue to discover the

33

French way of life and learn to appreciate the many ways the French view our world.

Cole Casper, Marketing and Communication Project Manager

REFERENCES

Boudreault, M. C., Cabirol, A., Trudeau, N., Poulin-Dubois, D., & Sutton, A. (2007). Les inventaires macarthur du développement de la communication: Validité et données normatives préliminaires. *Revue Canadienne d'orthophonie et d'audiologie, 31*(1), 27-37.

Brosseau-Lapré, F., & Rvachew, S. (2014). Cross-linguistic comparison of speech errors produced by English-and French-speaking preschool-age children with developmental phonological disorders. *International journal of speech-language pathology, 16*(2) 98-108.

David, A., & Wei, L. (2008). Individual differences in the lexical development of French-English bilingual children. *International Journal of Bilingual Education and Bilingualism, 11*(5), 598-618.

Desmarais, C., Sylvestre, A., Meyer, F., Bairati, I., & Rouleau, N. (2010). Three profiles of language abilities in toddlers with an expressive vocabulary delay: Variations on a theme. *Journal of Speech, Language and Hearing Research, 53*(3), 699.

IPA French (n.d.). In *Wikipedia*. (October 17, 2014). Retrieved at http://en.wikipedia.org/Help:IPA_for_French

Kayne, R. S. (1981). On certain differences between French and English. *Linguistic Inquiry, 12*(3), 349-371.

Lefebvre, P., Girard, C., Desrosiers, K., Trudeau, N., & Sutton, A. (2008). Phonological awareness tasks for French-speaking preschoolers. *Canadian Journal of Speech-Language Pathology and Audiology, 32*(6), 158-168.

MacLeod, A.A.N., Sutton, A., Sylvestre, A., Thordardottir, E., & Trudeau, N. (2014). Outil de dépistage des troubles du développement des sons de la parole: bases théoriques et données préliminaires. *Canadian Journal of Speech-Language Pathology and Audiology, 38*(1), 40-56.

Maillart, C., Schelstraete, M. A., & Hupet, M. (2004). Phonological representations in children with SLI: A study of french. *Journal of Speech, Language, and Hearing Research : JSLHR, 47*(1), 187-98.

Difference or Disorder?

Maillart, C., & Parisse, C. (2006). Phonological deficits in French-speaking children with SLI. *International Journal of Language & Communication Disorders, 41*(3), 253-74.

Parisse, C., & Maillart, C. (2008). Interplay between phonology and syntax in french-speaking children with specific language impairment. *International Journal of Language & Communication, 43*(4), 448-72.

Royle, P., & Valois, D. (2010). Acquisition of adjectives in quebec french as revealed by elicitation data. *Journal of French Language Studies, 20*(3), 313-338.

Rvachew, S., Marquis, A., Brosseau-Lapré, Paul, M. Royle, P., & Gonnerman, L. M. (2013). Speech articulation performance of francophone children in the early school years: Norming of the *Test de Depistage Francophone de Phonologie. Clinical Linguistics & Phonetics, 27*(12), 950-968.

Sylvestre, A., Desmarais, C., Meyer, F., Bairati, I., Rouleau, N., & Mérette, C. (2012). Factors associated with expressive and receptive language in french-speaking toddlers clinically diagnosed with language delay. *Infants & Young Children, 25*(2), 158-171.

Thordardottir, E. T. (2005). Early lexical and syntactic development in Quebec French and English : implications for cross-linguistic and bilingual assessment. *International Journal of Language & Communication Disorders, 40*(3), 243-278.

Thordardottir, E., Keheyia, E., Lessard, N., Sutton, A., & Trudeau, N. (2010). Typical performance on tests of language knowledge and language processing of french-speaking 5-year-olds. *Revue Canadienne D'orthophonie Et D'audiologie, 34*(1), 5-16.

U. S. Census Bureau (2010). 2010 Census Data. Retrieved at http://www.census.gov/2010census/data/

Chapter 7
German

"The limits of my language mean the limits of my world."

- Ludwig Wittgenstein

GENERAL INFORMATION

- **Number of speakers:** 123 million speakers worldwide

- **Writing system:** Latin alphabet; 26 standard letters plus three vowels with umlauts (Ä/ä, Ö/ö, and Ü/ü) and ß.

- **Language Family:** Indo-European—Germanic—West Germanic—High German

- **Official language in**: Germany, Switzerland, Austria, Liechtenstein, Luxembourg, Belgium, Italy (South Tyrol)

Difference or Disorder?

DEVELOPMENTAL NORMS FOR SPEECH

Age	Sounds
1;6-1;11	/p, m, d/
2;0-2;5	/b, n/
2;6-2;11	/ŋ, h, t, k, f, l, s, z, v, x/
3;0-3;5	/j, g, ʁ, pf/
3;6-3;11	/ts/
4;0-4;5	/ç/

(Fox, 2007; Fox & Dodd, 1999)
Note: Age range for 90% criterion mastery

DEVELOPMENTAL NORMS FOR PHONOLOGICAL PROCESSES

Age of Suppression	Phonological process
2;5	Replace /ʁ/ with glottal sound
2;11	Weak syllable deletion, Deaffrication
2;5 for /ŋ/, 3;5 for /k,g/	Fronting
3;11	Vocalization, Assimilation, Cluster reduction

(Fox, 2007; Schäfer & Fox, 2006)

PHONOLOGY AND PHONOTACTICS

Patterns of Native Language Influence:	Example:
Replacement of /w/ with /v/	want – vant
Replacement of /Ɵ/ with /t/ or /s/	thing – sing
Replacement of /ð / with /d/	that – dat
Devoicing of all final consonants	mad – mat
	bag – back

(Fox, 2007)
Note: In German, voiced consonants are always devoiced at the end of a word.

CONTRASTIVE ANALYSIS FOR SPEECH

Venn Contrast: German & English Consonant Phonemes

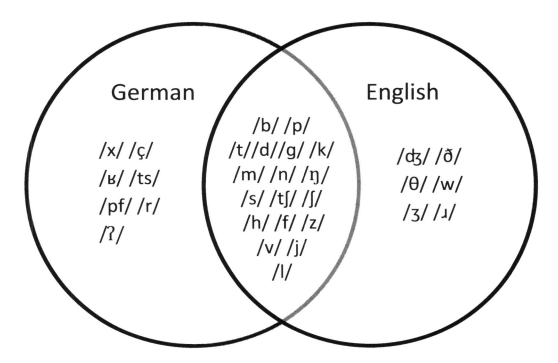

Venn Contrast: German & English Vowel Phonemes

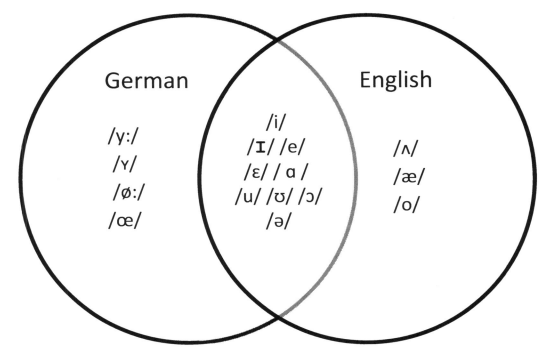

(Fox, 2007; IPA for German, n.d.; Maddieson, 1994)

Difference or Disorder?

CONTRASTIVE ANALYSIS FOR LANGUAGE: MORPHOSYNTAX

Note: Sentences marked with an asterisk (*) are not grammatical.

Feature			German	English	Examples of Errors
Word order			Flexible	Strict Subject-Verb-Object order	I threw over the fence some hay to the horse.*/I threw some hay to the horse over the fence.
Present tense verb use			Simple Present	Future, Present Progressive, or Simple Present	I eat my dinner now.*/I'm eating my dinner now.
Past tense verb use			Past Perfect	Simple Past or Past Perfect	Then I have drunk a soda.*/Then I drank a soda.
Question formation	Questions marked by inversion or question words	Word order inversion or addition of "do"	What means that word, please?*/What does that word mean, please?		

(Rintelman, 2012; Shoebottom, 2014)

SPECIAL NOTE: SEMANTICS

A German speaker acquiring English as a second language may make common word choice errors that reflect different concepts in their languages. This often results when, in one language, a single word represents a broader meaning than the rough translation equivalent in another language.

Vocabulary Word:	Examples of Errors:
"Schwer" = heavy/hard	The homework is very heavy.*/The homework is very hard.
"Aktuel" = current/actually	That's happening actually.*/That's happening currently.
"Ausleihen" = lend/borrow	Can I lend your pencil?*/Can I borrow your pencil?
"Erinern" = remember/remind	I don't remind.*/I don't remember.
"Aufgeregt" = excited/anxious	I'm anxious for Halloween.*/I'm excited for Halloween.
"Machen" = make/have/do	We will make a party.*/We will have a party.

HOME CORNER

Having two nationalities is something special. As a small child, one doesn't usually appreciate that. Having mastered German, I struggled at first to learn my second language, French, from my mother. The other children didn't have to learn another language. As I got older, however, I began to recognize the positive aspects of being bilingual and bicultural. I began to feel more at home in both France and Germany, even though, interestingly, I continued to feel a bit like a foreigner in both. I learned through time that it was possible to take the best of both cultures and unite them in my personality, which has been very enriching for me. From my perspective, this made me more open-minded and curious about new things. In today's multicultural environment, being bicultural is certainly an advantage in life because curiosity is the most important ingredient for success in discovering the world around you. Living in multiple cultures is the most unique adventure you can have in your life.

Mechanical Engineering student at the University of Austin at Austin, Texas

REFERENCES

Fox, A. (2007). German Speech Acquisition. In S. McLeod (ed.). *The International Guide to Speech Acquistion* (pp. 386-393). Clifton Park, NY: Thompson Delmar Learning.

Fox, A. V., & Dodd, B. J. (1999). Der Erwerb des phonologischen Systems in der deutschen Sprache. *Sprache – Stimme – Gehör,* 23, 183-191.

IPA for German (n.d.). In *Wikipedia*, (October 17, 2013). Retrieved from http://en.wikipedia.org/wiki/Help:IPA_for_German

Maddieson, I. (1984). (October 17, 2014). Native Phonetic Inventory: German. *The Speech Accent Archive,* Retrieved from http://accent.gmu.edu/browse_native.php?function=detail&languageid=24

Rintelman, Lauri. (2012, April 6). A Comparison of German and English. Retrieved from http://www.slideshare.net/LauriRintelman/a-comparison-of-german-and-english-12296261.

Difference or Disorder?

Schäfer, B., & Fox, A. V. (2006). Der Erwerb der Wortproduktionskonsequenz bei Zweijährigen: ein Mittel zur Früherkennung von Aussprachestörungen?. *Sprache· Stimme· Gehör, 30*(04), 186-192.

Shoebottom, Paul. (2014, June 2). The differences between English and German. Retrieved from http://esl.fis.edu/grammar/langdiff/german.htm.

Chapter 8
Hebrew

GENERAL INFORMATION

- **Number of speakers:** 5.3 million native speakers

- **Writing system:** Hebrew alphabet, 22 letters (5 of the letters have a different orthography when they are the final consonant); written from right to left

    o Derived from ancient Phoenician script called abjad. Only consonants are represented.

    o Nikud, or pointing, was introduced around 1000 years ago to indicate vowel values by means of dots placed underneath and to the side of the consonant letter. Dots inside certain letters distinguish stops from spirants or represent historical doubling (Coulmas, 2003; Shimrom, 1993). By second or third grade, children can read without the use of Nikud.

- **Language Family:** Afro-Asiatic—Semitic—Central Semitic—Northwest Semitic—Canaanite

- **Official language in**: Israel

Difference or Disorder?

Hebrew Alphabet

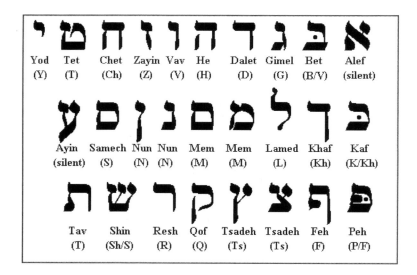

DEVELOPMENTAL NORMS FOR SPEECH

Age	Sounds
3;0	/p, b, m, n, j, f, x/
3;6	/k, l/
4;0	/t, g/
5;0	/d/
After 5;0	/s, ʃ, h, v, z/

(Ben-David & Berman, 2007; Lavie, 1978)

PHONOLOGY AND PHONOTACTICS

Patterns of Native Language Influence:	Example:
Replacement of voiceless th (θ) with /t/ or /s/ in all positions	thumb – tum mouth – mous
Replacement of voiced th (θ) with /d/ or /z/ in all positions	they – dey
Stress is usually on the ultimate or penultimate syllable in Hebrew. There is more variability in English.	uniVERsity – universiTY
Distortion of /ɹ/ distorted in all positions	
Confusion with /v/ and /w/	vacuum – wacuum wax - vax
Omission of initial glottal consonant	helping – elping
No long/short vowel discrimination	ship – sheep (or the other way around)

(Ben-David & Berman, 2007; Lavie, 1978)

CONTRASTIVE ANALYSIS FOR SPEECH

Venn Contrast: Hebrew & English Consonant Phonemes

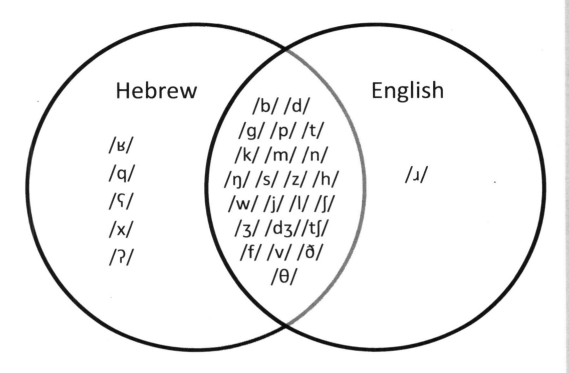

Venn Contrast: Hebrew & English Vowel Phonemes

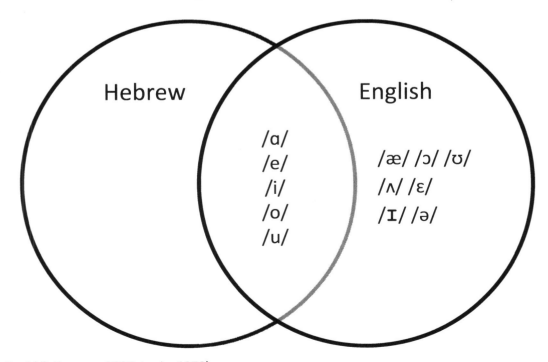

(Ben-David & Berman, 2007; Lavie, 1978)

Difference or Disorder?

CONTRASTIVE ANALYSIS FOR LANGUAGE: MORPHOSYNTAX

Note: Sentences marked with an asterisk (*) are not grammatical.

Feature	Hebrew	English	Examples of Errors
Word order	Flexible	Strict Subject Verb Object order	The ball he threw.*/ He threw the ball.
Copula *to be* in present tense	Does not exist	Mandatory	I tired.*/I am tired.
Adjectives	Adjective follows noun	Adjective precedes noun	The ball big*/ The big ball.
Verb inflection	Many forms, determined by person, gender, and number. highly inflected language	2 present tense forms: I eat You eat He/She/It eats We eat You all eat They eat	Omission of 3rd person "s": She talk to me.* / She talks to me.
Indefinite article	Does not exist	Exists	I have book.*/I have a book.
Question formation	Questions marked by inflection or question words	Word order inversion or addition of "do"	You give me a sticker?*/ Will you give me a sticker? What you think?*/ What do you think? We can go?* / Can we go?

(Coulmas, 2003; Tolchinsky, 2003)

HOME CORNER

Growing up in Israel we start learning English in the third grade. I was always good at it, but my parents thought that it wasn't enough and hired a tutor to teach me English. I also really liked watching movies – but I always hated reading subtitles since reading them makes you miss much of the movie – so I just ignored them and tried to understand what I could. At the age of 11, I went to the United States for the first time in order to visit my grandparents and, much to everyone's surprise, I could understand mostly everything and even communicate quite well! Two years later, I visited the United States again and by that point I already could speak freely and understand just about anything. I also acquired some friends around my age in the United States with whom I spent a lot of time, which allowed me to practice my spoken English. I kept visiting the United States every other year coupled with using English on a daily basis and on the internet. I feel very much at home when I need to write, read, or talk in English.

Shay Sudman, Student at Tel Aviv University

REFERENCES

Coulmas, F. (2003). Writing systems. *An introduction to their linguistic analysis, CUP.*

Ben-David, A., & Berman, R. A. (2007). Israeli Hebrew Speech Acquisition. In S. McLeod, The Internationa Guide tol Speech Acquisition (pp. 437-456). Clifton Park, NY: Thompson Delmar Learning.

Lavie, S. (1978). Norms for the development of Hebrew consonants between the ages of 3 to 5 years. [In Hebrew]. Unpublished master's thesis, Tel Aviv University.

Shimrom, J. (1993). The role of vowels in reading. A review of studies of English and Hebrew. *Psychological Bulletin, 114,* 52-67.

Tolchinsky, L. (2003). *The Cradle of Culture and What Children Know About Writing and Numbers Before Being.* Psychology Press.

Chapter 9
Japanese

GENERAL INFORMATION

- **Number of speakers:** More than 120 million speakers worldwide

- **Writing system:** The Japanese language was initially written entirely using adopted Chinese characters. These logographic Chinese characters are referred to as Chinese *kanji*. Apart from Chinese kanji, women developed *hiragana* as a cursive written form that was initially limited to their use only, and priests developed *katakana* as a phonetic reading of Chinese kanji.

  Japanese is made up of three orthographic systems: hiragana, katakana, and kanji.

  o Hiragana and katakana consist of 46 symbols made up of CV clusters, five vowels, and the letter *n*. Hiragana is used for inflections and bound morphemes. It is the first orthographic system children learn (Ota & Ueda, 2007).

  o Katakana symbols are similar to the hiragana symbols but are typically used for loanwords, onomatopoeia, and to emphasize words (Tohsaku, 2006).

- **Language Family:** The exact language family of Japanese is not known, and it is considered a language isolate; however, it has been theorized that Japanese belongs to the Ural-Altaic languages, or that it is closely related to Korean due to the similarities in grammar between the two languages.

- **Official Language in**: Japan and small Japanese communities in American Samoa, North America (Hawaii) and South America (Brazil), Europe, and Australia (Ota & Ueda, 2007)

DEVELOPMENTAL NORMS FOR SPEECH

Age	Sounds
2;0-2;3	/m, t, p, b, g, k, n/
2;4-2;7	/j, cɕ, d, w/
2;8-3;1	/ʥ, h/
3;2-3;5	/ɕ, r/
3;6-4;0	/ts, s, z, Φ/
After 4;0	/ç /

Based on many studies reported in Ota & Ueda, 2007.

DEVELOPMENTAL NORMS FOR PHONOLOGICAL PROCESSES

Age of suppression	Phonological process
4	Assimilation, Syllable reduction, Cluster reduction (C + /j/)
5	Stopping of fricatives, stopping of word-initial /r/ and rhoticization of word medial /d/, palatalization, deletion of /h/ and /r/, Velar fronting, backing of alveolars and palatals, metathesis

Based on many studies reported in Ota & Ueda, 2007.

There are numerous differences between Japanese and English that result in common cross-linguistic errors by English Language Learners (ELL). Differences may be seen in the areas of phonology, phonotactics, morphosyntax, and semantics.

48

Difference or Disorder?

CONTRASTIVE ANALYSIS FOR SPEECH

Venn Contrast: Japanese & English Consonant Phonemes

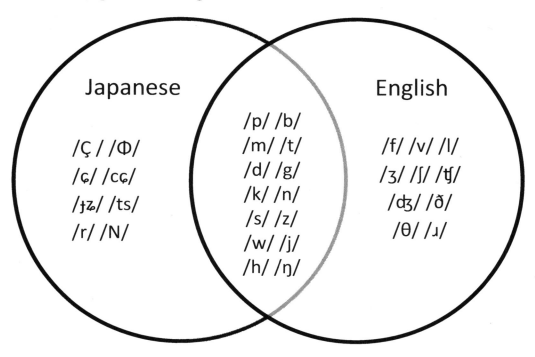

Venn Contrast: Japanese & English Vowel Phonemes

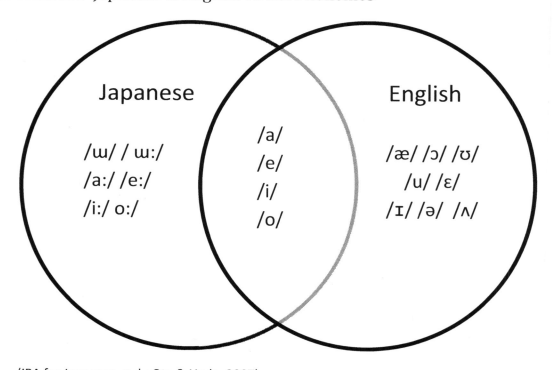

(IPA for Japanese, n.d.; Ota & Ueda, 2007)

PHONOLOGY AND PHONOTACTICS:

Patterns of Native Language Influence:	Examples:
Vowel distortions	slip – sleep
	test – taste
In Japanese, there are only five vowels. The five vowel sounds can be long or short. Long vowels are held twice as long as short vowels, but there is no pronunciation difference between long and short vowels.	stood – stewed
Multiple syllables accented	tsu-NA-mi – tsu-na-mi
All syllables in Japanese receive equal stress, whereas stress fluctuates in English words.	
Omission of word final consonants or addition of vowel after final consonant	chocolate – chocolato OR chocola
In Japanese, only 6 sounds appear at the end of words (5 vowels and /n/), whereas in English, many more consonants are allowed in this position.	
Consonant cluster reduction	store – tore
In Japanese, words do not start or end with consonant clusters. Syllables can be only one consonant, a consonant and one vowel, or a consonant plus a glide and a vowel. Additionally, there are special syllables consisting of /n/, double consonants, or double vowels.	
Addition of a vowel before /n/ in word- initial position	new – enew
In Japanese, a word cannot begin with the /n/ sound.	
Pronunciation of /n/ as /m/ before /m/, /p/, or /b/	pinball – pimball
Pronunciation of /n/ as /ng/ before a vowel, at the end of a word, or before /k/, /y/, /w/, /g/, or /ng/	won – wong
Devoicing of /ɪ/ or /u/ when occurring between two voiceless consonants, or at the end of the word with a preceding voiceless consonant	pursue – purs
In Japanese, this characteristic only occurs in running speech, but if the word is pronounced in isolation, these vowels may not be devoiced.	

Difference or Disorder?

Patterns of Native Language Influence:	Examples:
Omission or distortion of diphthongs	ride – rid
In Japanese, there are generally no diphthongs.	
English /r/ may sound like a combination of /r/ and /l/	rent – rlent
Non-labial consonants in front of /ɪ/ are palatalized	seat – sheet zero – zhero
Consonant /t/ in front of /ɪ/ and /u/ is palatalized and affricated	teacher – cheacher
/w/ may be omitted when it precedes any vowels except /a/	weather – ather

(Fengping, 2004; Ohata, 2004; Paul, Simons, & Fennig, 2014; Shizuo, Kakita, & Okada, 2011)

CONTRASTIVE ANALYSIS OF LANGUAGE: MORPHOSYNTAX

Note: Sentences marked with an asterisk (*) are not grammatical.

Feature	Japanese	English	Examples of Errors
Word order	Flexible	Strict Subject-Verb Object order	He ball threw.*/ He threw the ball.
Plurals	Do not exist	Exist	He bought three ball.*/ He bought three balls.
Auxiliary verbs	Do not exist	Exist	He walking.*/ He is walking.
Verbs inflection	A single form is used regardless of person or number	Two present tense forms.	She go.*/She goes. My father work.* /My father works.
Passive voice	Used in different circumstances and is constructed differently, which may result in word order errors	Object precedes verb and stating the subject is optional	The woman was cut his hair.*/His hair was cut by the woman.
Adjectives/adjectival phrases	Precede the nouns they modify (no matter how long the phrase)	Typically precede nouns, but may follow nouns	Faster than you he is.*/He is faster than you.
Articles	Do not exist	Exist	He threw ball.*/He threw the ball.
Relative pronouns	Do not exist	Exist	New in school teacher said hello.*/The teacher, who is new to the school, said hello.

Feature	Japanese	English	Examples of Errors
Personal/possessive Pronouns	Not always required	Always required	He took off glasses and brushed hair.*/He took off his glasses and brushed his hair.
Prepositions	Particles may be used to express the relationship between words	Specific words that precede a noun and its article	He brought a small dog of his.*/ He came with his dog.
Subject	Does not need to be restated if implied or has already been stated	Always required	Went to the store.*/I went to the store.

(Fengping, 2004; Paul, Simons, & Fennig, 2014; Power, 2008; Shoebottom, 2014; Vogler, 1998)

HOME CORNER

When I was an infant, my father had the opportunity to study as a post-doctoral fellow in the U.S. for four years. My mother, who was raised biculturally in China and Japan, so greatly regretted losing her Chinese language skills that she insisted that we spoke only in English so that when we returned to Japan, I would be well-grounded in the English language. Upon our return to Japan, she enrolled me in an American school so that I could continue my education in English. As a result, I had the opportunity of being raised bilingually/biculturally in an American school system in Japan. Although initially it was a shock to be in a country full of people speaking only in Japanese, and being exposed to English during the day at school, these very experiences are what have shaped me as an individual today.

I returned to the U.S. for university, then medical school, training and working as an emergency physician with the intent to stay in America. However, now with two young children of my own, I have decided to return to Japan, to give them the same opportunity that I had. Speaking more than one language and having exposure to different cultures not only is increasingly important in a globalized world, but also improves cognitive skills not

52

Difference or Disorder?

related to language. In addition, research shows that it may even shield against dementia later in life. I realize that giving my children a bilingual/bicultural experience is the best gift that I as a mother can give.

Minako Abe, E.R. Physician

REFERENCES

Fengping, G. (2004). Japanese culture and Japanese language—A comparative study on communication between Japanese and Non-Japanese. *The Journal of Nagasaki University of Foreign Studies, 8*, 147-163.

IPA for Japanese (n.d.). In Wikipedia. (October 17, 2014), Retrieved from http://en.wikipedia.org/wiki/Help:IPA_for_Japanese

Japanese language. (2014). In Encyclopaedia Britannica. Retrieved from http://www.britannica.com/EBchecked/topic/301146/Japanese-language

Maddieson, I. (1984). Native phonetic inventory: Japanese. In *The Speech Accent Archive,* Retrieved from http://accent.gmu.edu/browse_native.php?function=detail&languageid=33

Ohata, K. (2004). Phonological differences between Japanese and English: Several potentially problematic areas of pronunciation for Japanese ESL/EFL learners. *Asian EFL Journal, 6*(4).

Ota, M., & Ueda, I. (2007). Japanese Speech Acquisition. In S. McLeod (ed.). *The International Guide to Speech Acquisition*, Clifton Park, NY: Thompson Delmar Learning.

Paul, L., Simons, G. and Fennig, C. (2014). Ethnologue: Languages of the world (17th ed.). Dallas, Texas: SIL International. Online version: http://www.ethnologue.com.

Power, J. (2008). Japanese names. *The Indexer, 26*(2), C4-2-C4-8.

Shizuo, H., Kakita, K. & Okada, H. (2011). A panphonic version of the text of 'The North Wind and the Sun' for the illustration of the IPA of Japanese (Tokyo Dialect) Consonants. *The Journal of the Acoustical Society of America,* pp. 871-873.

Shoebottom, P. (2014). *The differences between Japanese and English.* Retrieved from http://esl.fis.edu/grammar/langdiff/japanese.htm

Tohsaku, Y. (2006). Yookoso! Continuing with Contemporary Japanese. Boston: McGraw Hill.

Vogler, D. (1998). *An overview of the history of the Japanese language.* Retrieved from http://linguistics.byu.edu/classes/ling450ch/reports/japanese.htm

Chapter 10
Korean

"Even though words have no wings, they can still fly a thousand miles."

- Korean Proverb

GENERAL INFORMATION

- **Number of speakers:** 78 million speakers worldwide; 42 million speakers in the Republic of Korea (South Korea), 20 million in Democratic People's Republic of Korea (North Korea); 1,141,277 speakers of Korean in the United States (U.S. Census, 2010)

- **Writing system:** In South Korea, the Korean alphabet is used as a primary written form and Chinese characters are used to provide additional meaning in some cases. In North Korea, there is no instruction in Chinese characters, and they are not used in newspapers, magazines, or books (Kim, 1987; Kim & Pae, 2007).

Difference or Disorder?

- **Language family:** Korean is currently considered a language isolate. Two of the more prominent theories about possible language families are referred to as the Southern Theory and the Northern Theory. The Southern Theory proposes that the Korean people and language originated in the South Pacific region and the Korean language is related to the Dravidian languages of India or to the Austronesian languages of Southeast Asia and the Pacific. The Northern Theory proposes that Korean is a member of the Altaic family (Kim, 1987; Kim & Pae, 2007).

- **Official language in:** South Korea, North Korea

DEVELOPMENTAL NORMS FOR SPEECH

Age	Sound
2	/p*, ph, t*, h/
3	/k*, th, p, m, t, n, ŋ, tɕ, tɕ*, tɕh /
4	/k, kh/
5	/l/
6	/s, s*/

The sound is produced with greater articulatory strength.

(Kim, 1996; Kim & Pae, 2005; Oum, 1994)

PHONOLOGY AND PHONOTACTICS

Patterns of Native Language Influence:	Example:
Replacement of /b/ with /p/ [b] exists as an allophone of /p/ in Korean, but never appears in word initial position.	bear - pear
Replacement of /f/ with /p/	feel - peal
Replacement of /v/ with /b/	van - ban
Omission or distortion of /z/	he's - he (verb omission error) peas -pea (plural error) zoo – choo

Patterns of Native Language Influence:	Example:
Replacement of /ʃ/ with /s/	she – see
Replacement of /tʃ/ with "ts"	beach – beets
Replacement of /ɹ/ with /l/	rice – lice
Replacement of /æ/ with /ɛ/	hem for ham
Replacement of /θ/ with /s/	thick – sick
Addition of /ɪ/ or /ə/ at end of word	church – churchy or churchuh
Only seven consonants occur in syllable-final position: /p, t, k, m, n, ŋ, l/. Fricatives and affricates never appear in word-final position.	
Nasalization of final stops preceding a nasal sound	I took mom home-I toong mom home
Allophonic variations may result in errors for sounds in certain positions.	packet-pagget apple-abble
/p, t, k/ become voiced stops [b, d, g] between sonorant phonemes.	
Omission, addition, or distortion of sounds in a word-initial or word-final consonant clusters Consonant clusters only occur in inter-syllabic positions.	clap – cuh-lap

(Kim, 2006; Oum, 1994)

CONTRASTIVE ANALYSIS FOR SPEECH

Venn Contrast: Korean & English Consonant Phonemes

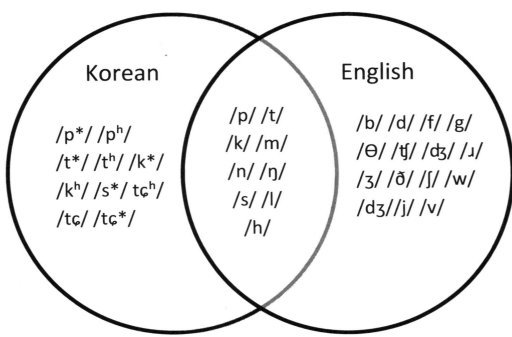

Korean: /p*/ /pʰ/ /t*/ /tʰ/ /k*/ /kʰ/ /s*/ tɕʰ/ /tɕ/ /tɕ*/

Shared: /p/ /t/ /k/ /m/ /n/ /ŋ/ /s/ /l/ /h/

English: /b/ /d/ /f/ /g/ /ɵ/ /ʧ/ /ʤ/ /ɹ/ /ʒ/ /ð/ /ʃ/ /w/ /dʒ/ /j/ /v/

* represents greater articulatory strength; /l/ and /r/ are allophones in Korean

Venn Contrast: Korean & English Vowel Phonemes

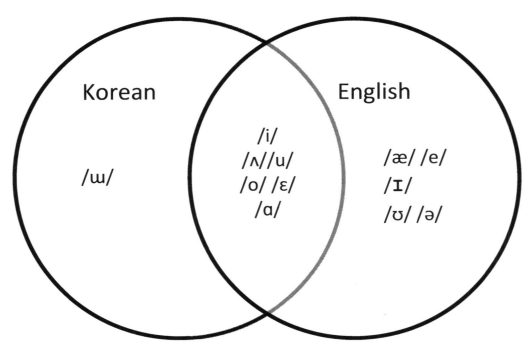

Korean: /ɯ/

Shared: /i/ /ʌ/ /u/ /o/ /ɛ/ /ɑ/

English: /æ/ /e/ /ɪ/ /ʊ/ /ə/

(Jun, 2007; Kim, 2009; Kim & Pae, 2007)

CONTRASTIVE ANALYSIS OF LANGUAGE: MORPHOSYNTAX

Feature	Korean	English	Examples of Errors
Word order	SOV	SVO	I food eat.*/I eat food.
Articles	Do not exist	Definite (the) and indefinite (a, an)	Cat is brown. / The cat is brown.
Prepositions	Do not exist	Exist	She lives parents.*/She lives with her parents.
Third person pronoun	3rd person pronoun does not mark gender	Masculine, feminine and neuter pronoun used	He is my mother.*/She is my mother.
Pronoun use	Repeat noun rather than use pronoun	Replace noun with pronoun	John goes to school, and John studies every day.*/John goes to school, and he studies every day.
Adjectives	Adjective always comes before the word it modifies	Adjective usually comes before the word it modifies but not always	This is pretty something.*/This is something pretty.
Passive voice	The same form is used for active and passive meanings	Different forms are used for active and passive meanings	The party was bored.*/The party was boring.
Direct object pronouns	Not required	Required	Yes, I want.*/Yes, I want some.
Modifiers	Placed between verb and direct object	Placed after direct object	She speaks very well English.*/She speaks English very well.
Singular vs. plural	Nouns are not marked for number	Nouns are marked for number	I like comedy movies.*/I like comedy movie.
Subject/verb agreement	Not required	Required	He go to work every day.*/He goes to work every day. John and Sarah has a new dog.*/John and Sarah have a new dog.
Past tense verb forms	Do not exist	Exist	I eat pizza yesterday.*/I ate pizza yesterday.
Future tense verbs	Present tense is used to talk about the future	Has future tense verb form	I come next week.*/I will come next week.
Auxiliary verbs	Do not exist in negative statements	Exist in negative statements	I no understand.*/I do not understand.
Present progressive verb forms	Do not exist	Exist	Stop talk.*/Stop talking.
"If" vs. "When"	Same word	Different meanings	If you arrive, call me.*/When you arrive, call me.

Difference or Disorder?

Feature	Korean	English	Examples of Errors
Stress patterns	Stress does not differentiate word meaning	Stress may differentiate word meaning	"Record" is produced with equal stress for reCORD (verb) and REcord (noun).*
Questions	Do not add modals	Add modals	Where you went?*/Where did you go?
	No subject-verb inversion	Use subject-verb inversion	He goes to work with you?*/Does he go to work with you?
	Answer Yes/No questions by repeating verb	Use "Yes" or "No" to answer Yes/No question	Q: Do you want more juice? A: I want.*/Yes.

(Cheng, 1991; Farvor, Kim, & Lee, 1995; Farver & Shinn, 1997; Opitz, Rubin, & Erekson, 2011; Pae, 1995)

HOME CORNER

The most memorable thing for me was when I came back to the United States for high school. I transferred directly from a strict all-girls middle school in Korea to a co-ed high school. In my first English class, my teacher put his foot up on my desk as he was leaning in his chair. I was shocked, as this was a sign of disrespect in Korea. I was also taught not to speak up to the teachers so I kept quiet. I looked at him with surprise as he winked at me and started to introduce himself. Winking was a bit too much for my 13-year-old self who just came out of an all-girls middle school. I was extremely uncomfortable for the rest of the class. However, after a year, as I became more accustomed to the culture, he and I became good friends. We joked about how awkward I felt in that first day of class, and he would sometimes put his foot up on my desk and wink at me as a running joke.

I really think this stands as a great representation of me becoming more accustomed to American culture. I was fortunate enough to find a teacher that was humorous, kind, and helpful.

Jin Kwon, Speech-Language Pathologist

59

REFERENCES

Cheng, L. (1991). Assessing Asian language performance: Guidelines for evaluating limited-English proficient students (2nd ed.). Oceanside, CA: Academic Communication Associates.

Farver, J. M., Kim, Y. K., & Lee, Y. (1995). Cultural differences in Korean- and Anglo-American preschoolers' social interaction and play behaviors. *Child Development, 66,* 1088-1099.

Farver, J. M., & Shinn, Y. L. (1997). Social pretend play in Korean- and Anglo- American pre-schoolers. *Child Development, 68* (3), 544-556.

Jun, S. (2007). Phonological Development of Korean: A case study. *Working Papers in Phonetics, 105,* 51-65.

Kim, M. (2006). Phonological error patterns of preschool children for 'Korean Test of Articulation and Phonology for Children' [In Korean]. *Korean Journal of Communication Disorders, 11* (2), 17-31.

Kim, M. and Pae, S. (2005). The percentage of consonants correct and the ages of consonantal acquisition for "Korean Test of Articulation for Children" [in Korean]. *Korean Journal of Speech Sciences, 12(2),* 139-152.

Kim, M., & Pae, S. (2007). Korean speech acquisition. In S. McLeod, *The International Guide to Speech Acquisition* (pp. 472-482). Clifton Park: Thomson Delmar Learning.

Kim, Y. (2009). Crosslinguistic influence on phonological awareness for Korean-English bilingual children. *Reading and Writing, 22,* 843-861.

Kim, Y. (1996). The percentage of consonants correct (PCC) using picture articulation test in preschool children. *Korean Journal of Speech and Hearing Disorders, 2,* 29-52.

Kim, N. (1987). Korean. *The World's Major Languages.* Bernard Comrie (ed.). Rutledge. London: Croom Helm.

Opitz, M. F., Rubin, D., & Erekson, J. A. (2011). Appendix C: Teacher's resource guide of language transfer issues for English language learners. In M. F. Opitz, D. Rubin, & J. A. Erekson, *For reading diagnosis and improvement.* Pearson.

Oum, J. (1994). Speech sound development: Three, four, and five year-old children [In Korean]. In Korean society of communication disorders (Ed.), *The treatment of articulation disorders for children (pp. 54-66). Seoul: Kunja Inc.*

Pae, S. (1995). The development of language in Korean children [In Korean]. In Korean society of communication disorders (Ed.), *Training of speech pathologists* (pp. 18-35). Seoul: Hanhaksa.

U. S. Census Bureau (2010). 2010 Census Data. Retrieved from http://www.census.gov/2010census/data/

Chapter 11
Mandarin

GENERAL INFORMATION

- **Number of speakers:** 2.5 million speakers of Chinese languages (includes Mandarin, Cantonese, Hakka, etc.) in the United States (U.S. Census, 2010)

- **Writing system:** Pinyin

- **Language Family:** Sino—Tibetan—Sinitic

- **Official language in**: Major cities of northern and southwestern China; Taiwan

DEVELOPMENTAL NORMS FOR SPEECH

Age	Sounds
1;6-2;0	/m, t, tʰ, n, x/
2;1-2;6	/p, pʰ, ɕ, tɕ, tɕʰ, k, kʰ/
2;7-3;0	/f/
3;7-4;0	/l, s, ʂ, ʐ, tɕ, tɕʰ/
>4;6	/ts, tsʰ, ʂ/

(Hua, 2007; Hua & Dodd, 2000)

SPECIAL NOTE: TONAL LANGUAGES

Mandarin is a tonal language; the written characters are phonetically represented by both a single syllable and a tonal marker. Mandarin has four distinct tones and one neutral tone. Tonal markers are produced using intonation contours, the rise and fall of pitch, across the syllable. It is this combination of phonemes (segmental features) and intonation (suprasegmental features) that provides meaning to a syllable. If both aspects of the syllable are not produced correctly, a completely different word meaning can be understood. Individual characters can be used in either isolation or in combination to form semantic representations. The same phonological representation is used, whether the written symbol is a Chinese character or the Pinyin word. Pinyin is a transcription of Chinese characters using a Roman alphabetical system and is used to represent words in a semi-phonological manner with markers to indicate the suprasegmental/tonal features. For example, the word "that" is represented in standard Chinese by the character 那 in Pinyin, "náh" in Mandarin, and "nà" in Cantonese.

Syllable	Tone Level	Tone Description	Word Meaning
Mā	1	High-level	Mother
Má	2	Rising	Hemp
Mǎ	3	Falling-rising	Horse
Mà	4	Falling	To scold

(Cheng, 1991; Hua & Dodd, 2000)

The influences of the tonal aspect and monosyllabic/bisyllabic nature of Mandarin can result in difficulty producing intonation patterns when speaking English. The production of polysyllabic words can result in omission of syllables or inaccurate syllable stress patterns. These difficulties can also be seen across entire sentence level intonation contours, resulting in what can be described as "sounding monotone to the ears of Standard American English

Difference or Disorder?

speakers" (Fung & Roseberry-McKibbin, 1999). Only /m/ and /ŋ/ are permitted in word final position in Mandarin, which leads to the substitution or omission of sounds in at the ends of words in English, which permits many different sounds in word final position (Hua, 2007). There are no consonant clusters in Mandarin, while English has many consonant clusters. The result is often a reduction of consonant clusters to a single consonant sound, or sometimes a complete omission of the consonant cluster.

PHONOLOGY AND PHONOTACTICS

Patterns of Native Language Influence:

Pattern:	Example:
Omission of final consonants or substitution of /m/ or /ŋ/ in final position	cup – cu ton-toŋ
Devoicing of phonemes	dog – tog
Confusion between /l/ and /r/	lamp – ramp
Confusion between /tʃ/and /ʃ/	children – shildren
Addition of a neutral vowel such as /ə/ between consonants in a cluster	play – puhlay
Reduction of a consonant cluster to a single consonant	play – pay
Omission of a consonant cluster	central – cenal
Substitution of [θ] with [s]	thin – sin
Lengthening of the short vowels of English (/æ/ /ʌ/ /ʊ/ /ɪ/)	give – geev

(Hua, 2007; Hua & Dodd, 2000; Peña-Brooks & Hegde, 2007)

CONTRASTIVE ANALYSIS FOR SPEECH

Venn Contrast: Mandarin & English Consonant Phonemes

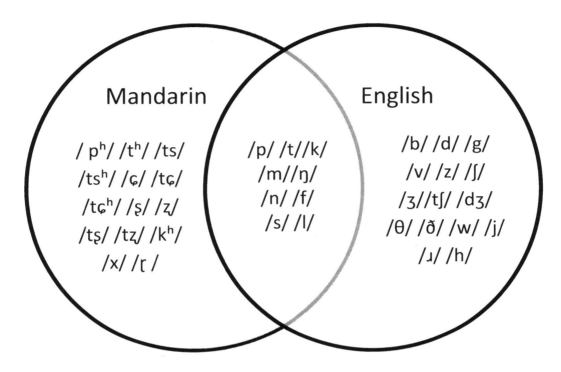

Venn Contrast: Mandarin & English Vowel Phonemes

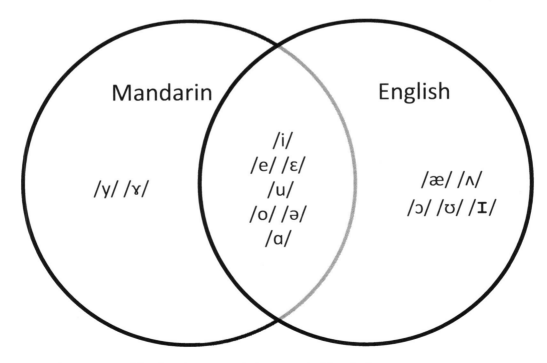

(Hua, 2007). Some consider ü to be a vowel phoneme in Mandarin.

Difference or Disorder?

CONTRASTIVE ANALYSIS FOR LANGUAGE: MORPHOSYNTAX

Feature	Mandarin	English	Examples of Errors
Pronoun	Neither gender nor case (e.g. subject vs. object) are differentiated.	Subject pronouns: he/she/they/we	Me mom is here.*/ My mom is here.
		Object pronouns: him/her/them/us	Them go to school.*/They go to school.
		Possessive pronouns: my/your/his/her	That him car.* / That's his car.
Articles	Does not use articles	Has definite (*the*) and indefinite (*a, an*) articles	I have cat.*/I have a cat.
Conjunctions	Usually conjoins ideas by juxtaposing related sentences	Usually conjoins ideas with a conjunction word	Mary ate dinner. Mary was hungry.*/Mary ate dinner because she was hungry.
Adjectives	Adjective follows noun	Adjective precedes noun	The ball red is deflate.*/The red ball is deflated.
			The car clean.*/The clean car.
Plurality	No plural markers	Add an /s/ to the noun	I want two sandwich.*/I want two sandwiches.
Verb conjugations	Verbs do not conjugate to show change in tense	Verb conjugates to demonstrate tense changes	I am eat.*/I am eating.
			She eat.*/She ate.
			The boy read.*/The boy will read.
Auxiliary verbs and the copula (to be)	Do not exist	Do exist	I sick.*/I'm sick.

Note: Sentences marked with an asterisk (*) are not grammatical.
(Li & Thompson, 1981; Ross, 1978)

HOME CORNER

I am a master's level student majoring in speech-language pathology and also a

sequential Mandarin-English bilingual speaker. I grew up in Taipei, Taiwan, and finished my undergraduate schooling there. I began learning English when I was 10 years old, but not until I came to the U.S. for my master's program did I truly understand what "English" is. When I first went to a party here, I did not understand any words that my classmates were speaking, even though I had been studying English for over 10 years. I felt frustrated and frightened by the idioms and fast speech rate. However, it is also my classmates who helped me overcome my fear of English vocabulary and American culture.

As a speech-language pathology student, I was required to dramatically improve my English skills in a short period of time. Therefore, I tried various strategies to polish my English and looked for opportunities to practice. I also participated in an accent modification rotation in our clinic to change my accent and intonation. This experience not only helped me improve the language but also let me understand how it feels to be a client sitting in the therapy room. As a matter of fact, when my professors were talking about the clients' perspectives and speech and language struggles, I was thrilled and surprised because I could empathize. It is exactly how I felt when I went to a party where communication made no sense to me, and I did not even have the ability to ask for help.

I am fortunate to be supported by so many people. This has increased my determination to be a bilingual speech-language pathologist. I am also grateful to be a bilingual speaker as well as a second-language learner and hope to build a bridge between two cultures. I appreciate that I have this opportunity to be immersed in different languages and cultures, and I've never felt negative towards choosing a profession that makes me confront so many language challenges. After all, these challenges have prepared me for being a bilingual speech-language pathologist and have made me more qualified to provide clients valid resources and feedback about the impact of being bilingual.

Min-An Song

Speech-Language Pathology Graduate Student

66

Difference or Disorder?

REFERENCES

Cheng, L. (1991). Assessing Asian language performance: Guidelines for evaluating limited-English proficient students (2nd ed.). Oceanside, CA: Academic Communication Associates.

Fung, F., & Roseberry-McKibbin, C. (1999). Service delivery considerations in working with clients from Cantonese-speaking backgrounds. *American Journal of Speech-Language Pathology, 8*, 309-318.

Hua, Z. (2007). Putonghua (Modern Standard Chinese). In S. McLeod, *The International Guide to Speech Acquisition* (pp. 516-527). Clifton Park, NY: Thompson Delmar Learning.

Hua, Z. & Dodd, B. (2000). Phonological Acquisition of Putonghua. *Journal of Child Language, 27*, 3-42.

Li, C. & Thomspon, S. (1981). An exploration of Mandarin Chinese. In Lehman, W.P. (Ed.), *Syntactic typology: Studies in the phenomenology of language.* (2nd ed.) Austin, TX: The University of Texas Press. Retrieved February 25, 2011 from http://www.utexas.edu/cola/centers/lrc/books

Peña-Brooks, A. & Hegde, M.N. (2007). *Assessment and treatment of articulation and phonologic disorders in children* (2nd ed.). Austin, TX: Pro-Ed, Inc.

Ross, C. (1978). Constraints on contrast conjoining: English and Mandarin Chinese. *Cahiers de linguistique-Asie orientale, 4*(1), 23-42.

Tao, F. (2007, March 7). More than half of Chinese speak Mandarin. Xinhua News Agency, Retrieved February 25, 2011, from http://news.xinhuanet.com/english

U. S. Census Bureau (2010). 2010 Census Data. Retrieved at http://www.census.gov/2010census/data/

Chapter 12
Russian

GENERAL INFORMATION

- **Number of speakers:** 160 million native speakers and 125 million speakers of Russian as a second language

- **Writing system:** Cyrillic script, 33 letters.

А а	Б б	В в	Г г	Д д	Е е	Ё ё	Ж ж
A a	B b	V v	G g	D d	Yeh yeh	Yo yo	Zh zh

З з	И и	Й й	К к	Л л	М м	Н н	О о
Z z	Ee ee	Ih ih	K k	L l	M m	N n	O o

П п	Р р	С с	Т т	У у	Ф ф	Х х	Ц ц
P p	R r	S s	T t	U u	F f	X x	Tz tz

Ч ч	Ш ш	Щ щ	ъ ы ь	Э э	Ю ю	Я я
Ch ch	Sh sh	Shch shch	- ih -	Eh eh	Yu yu	Ya ya

- **Language Family:** Indo-European—Balto-Slavic—Slavic—East Slavic

- **Official language in:** Russian Federation, Belarus, Ukraine, Kazakhstan, Kyrgyzstan

- **Unofficial yet still spoken in:** Moldova, Latvia, Lithuania, Estonia, Georgia, Armenia, Azerbaijan, Uzbekistan, Tajikistan

Difference or Disorder?

DEVELOPMENTAL NORMS FOR SPEECH

Age	Sounds
6-8 mo	Canonical babbling
8-12 mo	Variegated babbling
1;8	/m, p, b, k, g, dʲ, tʲ, nʲ, lʲ, sʲ, Xʲ, tsʲ/, consonant clusters in the medial position emerge (/lʲk, sʲk, pʲk, tzʲk/)
1;10-2;0	/n, t, d/
2;0-2;6	/s, l, v, r/
2;6-3;0	/ʧ, ʃ, ʒ, ts/

(Logoped, 2005; Povalyaeva, 2004; Gildersleeve-Neumann & Wright, 2010)

DEVELOPMENTAL NORMS FOR PHONOLOGICAL PROCESSES

Age of Suppression	Phonological process
1;8	Initial and/or final consonant deletion
1;10-2;0	Consonant cluster reduction, metathesis
2;0-2;6	Assimilation, elision, metathesis
2;6-3;0	Assimilation decreasing, metathesis
3;0-7;0	No phonological processes should exist except for occasional metathesis

(Logoped, 2005; Povalyaeva, 2004)

PHONOLOGY AND PHONOTACTICS

Patterns of Native Language Influence:	Example:
Replacement of voiceless "th" (θ) with /t/ or /s/ in all positions or /f/ in the final position	thumb – tum mouth – mous OR mout
Replacement of voiced "th" (ð) with /d/ or /z/ in all positions	they – dey
Replacement of /w/ with /v/ or /u/	west – vest
Omission of /g/ or replace /g/ with /k/ at the end of a word	sing – sin OR sink
Distortion of English "r" in all positions, often resembling a trill /r/ or tap /ɾ/	rabbit – rrrabbit
Replacement of /h/ with glottal fricative /x/	hat – /xat/
Short English vowels that do not occur in Russian may be substituted with a long vowel equivalent	witch – weetch
Devoicing of voiced fricatives and plosives in word final position	knob -- nop

(Gildersleeve-Neumann & Wright, 2010; Povalyaeva, 2004)

CONTRASTIVE ANALYSIS FOR SPEECH

Venn Contrast: Russian & English Consonants Phonemes

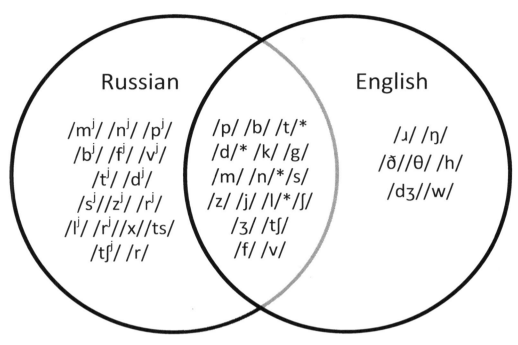

Phonemes marked with an asterisk (*) are always dentalized in Russian. The following sounds also occur in Russian but are considered by most linguists to be allophones rather than phonemes: kʲ, gʲ, xʲ, ʒʲ, ɣ, dz, d͡ʒʲ.

Venn Contrast: Russian & English Vowel Phonemes

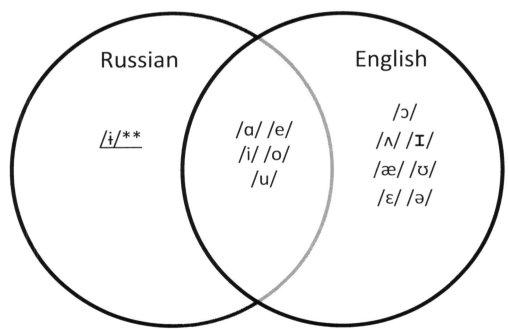

(Gildersleeve-Neumann & Wright, 2010; Hamilton, 1980; Kedrova, et al., 2002, Ladefoged, 2014)
** There is controversy about whether [ɨ] is a phoneme or an allophone of [i] in Russian.

Difference or Disorder?

DEVELOPMENTAL NORMS FOR LANGUAGE

Age	Feature
1-2	Vocabulary: nouns, verbs, adjectives, pronouns, adverbs.
1;6-	Vocabulary: ~ 27 words, more nouns than verbs
1;10	Syntax: 2-word utterances
1;10-2	Morphology: emerging adjective agreement; omission of 3rd person singular agreement; Syntax: 2-3 word utterances, mostly not grammatical
2-2;6	Vocabulary: acquire more adjectives and adverbs Syntax: 2-3 word utterances with conjugated verbs Morphology: emerging suffixes and indicative mood.
2-3	Vocabulary: emerging synonyms and antonyms, multiple meaning words, part-whole relationships, emerging prepositions (e.g. in, on, with) and conjunctions (e.g. because, so that, when), errors with possessives and pronouns Morphology: Emerging first case, mixing noun endings, expansion of inflections, emerging gender agreement. Syntax: Developing compound and complex sentences, developing noun-adjective agreement.
3-4	Vocabulary: mastery of comparatives, inconsistent use of prepositions Morphology: emerging declensions, developing verb endings including imperative endings, varied types of declinations and conjugations, errors with neuter adjective agreement Syntax: developing compound sentences Connected speech: development of connected speech and dialogues, simple story retells in egocentric speech
3-7	Vocabulary: development of synonyms and antonyms, multiple meaning words, and part-whole relationships.
4-6	Syntax: continue to exhibit errors Morphology: most grammatical forms acquired, all declination types mastered Connected speech: retell reading/story to adult, egocentric speech, create own stories and poems
5-7	Morphology: deviant declension of numerals, occasional participles

(Logoped, 2005; Povalyaeva, 2004)

SPECIAL NOTE: PALATIZATION

Most Russian consonants (stops, nasals, lateral, trill, and five of eight fricatives) are differentiated by a palatalization feature. This contrast of soft (palatalized) versus hard (non-palatalized) consonants is one of the most important aspects of Russian phonology (Zharkova, 2005). Soft consonants are produced with the tongue high in the mouth, near the palate. Hard consonants are produced with the tongue lower in the mouth. This distinction adds a level of complexity to the Russian consonant system that does not exist in English. A

Russian-speaking learner of English may palatalize consonants in English due the influence of this part of Russian phonology.

SPECIAL NOTE: CASE

In Russian, nouns and pronouns have many different forms. These morphological forms are called *cases*. Case is a grammatical category that reflects what role a noun plays in a sentence. Many languages use a variety of cases. There are six cases in Russian: nominative, genitive, accusative, dative, prepositional, and instrumental.

Case name	Used to mark...	Example
Nominative	subject of a verb	**The boy** is playing.
Genitive	possession	The leg **of the table** broke OR the **table's** leg broke.
Accusative	direct object of a verb	I saw **the painting**.
Dative	indirect object of a verb	I gave the letter **to my friend**.
Prepositional	object of a preposition	He thinks about **the homework**.
Instrumental	an object used to perform an action	I cut with **scissors**.

Russian nouns and pronouns undergo morphological changes depending on case and number. The inflection of nouns in this way is called *declension*. The bolded parts of the sentences above would be translated into Russian as one word with a special ending that indicates case. Research on crosslinguistic transfer in bilinguals indicates that sometimes case markers are carried over into one's second language in the acquisition process (Jarvis & Odlin, 2000; Zaretsky & Bar-Shalom, 2000). An example of crosslinguistic transfer would be the addition of "a" or "om" to an English noun (e.g. balla or ballom).

Difference or Disorder?

CONTRASTIVE ANALYSIS FOR LANGUAGE: MORPHOSYNTAX

Feature	Russian	English	Examples of Errors
Aspect	Add affixes to verb stem	Auxiliary verbs and copulas	He give his all.*/ He has given his all. He sleeping.*/He is sleeping She good teacher.*/She is a good teacher.
Gender	Present – masculine, feminine, neuter	Absent	He is comfortable.*/It is comfortable. – when referring to a chair.
Word order	Free	Strict Subject-Verb-Object order	The ball he threw.*/ He threw the ball.
Articles	No definite or indefinite articles	Must include definite or indefinite article	My mom gave me ball.*/ My mom gave me the ball.
Prepositions	Not as important because of case system	Increased importance and used more frequently	She explained me matter.*/She explained the matter to me.
Question formation	Questions marked by inflection or question words	Word order inversion or addition of "do"	You give me a sticker?*/ Will you give me a sticker? What you think?*/ What do you think? We can go?* / Can we go?

Note: Sentences marked with an asterisk (*) are not grammatical.

SPECIAL NOTE: PREPOSITIONS

Due to the frequency of preposition errors produced by Russian speakers acquiring English, a few specific examples are provided below to assist in identifying second language influenced errors.

Russian	English	Possible misuses of prepositions in L2 (English)
зависеть от (depend from)	depend on	She **depends from** me.
отказаться от (refuse from)	refuse __	They **refuse from** doing it.
готовиться к (prepare to)	prepare for	We will **prepare to** the party.
устал от (tired from)	tired of	I'm **tired from** doing this.
закончить ___ (finish ___)	graduate from university	I **graduated** university in 2010.
разделить на (divide on)	divide into	I will **divide on** two pieces.
ждать ___ (wait ___)	wait for someone	He is **waiting** his sister.
слушать ___ (listen___)	listen to music	I'm **listening** music.
объяснять ___ (explain___)	explain to someone	**Explain** me this problem.

HOME CORNER

From what I remember, it was always very important to me that I came from a Russian-speaking and culturally Russian background. This helped me feel "special" and distinct from my classmates, which I appreciated, and was one reason I never went through the "refusing-to-speak-the-native-language" period that kids go through when they want to fit in. I became pretty fluent in English and lost my accent by around fourth or fifth grade. English is my stronger language now, but Russian remains a big part of my life and identity. I learned how to read and write from my grandmother, and often did and do read in Russian. For me the contribution of Russian movies, books, jokes, and other cultural products, and of course socializing with actual Russian-speaking people, is very significant. One interesting thing was how my brother and I gradually shifted to English as the more comfortable, friendly language to use with each other, though we always code-switch a lot, while continuing to speak Russian-only to our parents.

Mariya Blokh, M.A., Speech-Language Pathologist

REFERENCES

Gildersleeve-Neumann, C. E., & Wright, K. L. (2010). English speech acquisition in 3- to 5-year-old children learning Russian and English. *Language, Speech, and Hearing Services in Schools, 41*, 429–444.

Grossman, J. D. (2014). Language development of bilingual Russian/English speaking children living in the United States: A review of the literature. *Honors Theses*, Paper 365.

Hamilton, W. S. (1980). *Introduction to Russian phonology and word structure.* Columbus, OH: Slavika Publishers.

Jarvis, S., & Odlin, T. (2000). Morphological type, spatial reference, and language transfer. *Studies in Second Language Acquisition, 22*(04), 535-556.

Kedrova, G. E., Potapov, V. V., Egorov, A. M., & Omelyanova, E. V. (2002). *Educational materials on Russian phonology.* (October 22, 2014), Retrieved from http://www.philol.msu.ru.rus/galya-1/index.htm

Difference or Disorder?

Ladefoged, P. (2014). *A Course in Phonetics* (5th ed.). Forth Worth, TX: Harcourt Brace Jovanovich.

Logoped (2005). Rechevoi ontogeniz: Vzglad lingvista [Speech ontogenesis: A linguistic overview]. *Logoped* [Speech language pathologist], *4*, 1-4.

Povalyaeva, M.A. (2004). Cpravochnik logopeda [Speech language pathologist directory]. Retrieved from: http://www.razlib.ru/medicina/ spravochnik_logopeda/index.php

Zaretsky, E. & Bar-Shalom, E. G. (2010). Does reading shallow LI orthography slow attrition of language-specific morphological structures? *Clinical Linguistics & Phonetics, 24*, (4-5), 401-415.

Zharkova, N. (2005). Strategies in the acquisition of segments and syllables in Russian-speaking children. *Leiden Papers in Linguistics*, *2* (189-213).

Chapter 13
Spanish

GENERAL INFORMATION

- **Number of speakers:** More than 405 million speakers worldwide; 37 million speakers above the age of 5 in the United States (U.S. Census, 2010)

- **Writing system:** Roman script, 27 letters and 3 digraphs ("ch," "ll," and "rr")

- **Language Family:** Indo-European—Italic—Romance

- **Official language in:** Spain, Colombia, Uruguay, Venezuela, Peru, Ecuador, Guatemala, Nicaragua, Cuba, Bolivia, Honduras, Paraguay, El Salvador, Costa Rica, Panama, Equatorial Guinea, Puerto Rico, Mexico, Chile, Argentina, Dominican Republic

DEVELOPMENTAL NORMS FOR SPEECH

Age	Sounds
3	/m, b, p/
4	/k, l, w, y, t, f, n/
5	/r, g, d, ɲ, ʧ/
6	/x, s/
7	/r/

Note: This information is based on the age at which 90% mastery is expected.
(Acevedo, 1992; Jimenez, 1987)

Difference or Disorder?

DEVELOPMENTAL NORMS FOR PHONOLOGICAL PROCESSES

Age of Suppression	Phonological process
3	Final Consonant Deletion, Medial Consonant Deletion, Weak Syllable Deletion, Initial Consonant Deletion, Fronting, Assimilation, Backing
5	Gliding, Cluster Reduction, Stopping, Liquid Simplification, Flap/Trill Deviation

(Bedore et al., 2007; Fabiano and Goldstein, 2010; Goldstein and Iglesias, 2006)

PHONOLOGY AND PHONOTACTICS

Patterns of Native Language Influence:	Example:
Replacement of voiceless "th" (/θ/) with /t/ or /s/ in all positions	thumb – tum mouth – mous
Replacement of voiced "th" (/ð/) with /d/ in all positions	they – dey
Replacement of /z/ with /s/ in all positions.	buzz – bus
Replacement of "sh" with "ch" or vice-versa in all positions	shoe – choe chicken – shicken watches – washes
Replacement of /v/ with /b/ in all positions	very – bery
Replacement of "j" with "y" or vice-versa in initial position	jello – yellow
Distortion of /ɹ/ in all positions, often resembling a trilled /r/ in initial position	/r/ distortion
Devoicing or omission of final consonants In Spanish, only 5 consonant sounds (r, s, l, n, d) appear at the end of words, whereas in English, more consonants are allowed in word final position, including consonant clusters, such as /kst/ in "mixed" and /ŋz/ in "meetings."	dog – doc mixed – miss
Omission or distortion of final consonant clusters. Spanish syllables are mostly consonant-vowel (CV), and clusters usually only have two consonants. In English, syllable shapes are more varied and clusters can have up to three consonants, such as /str/ in "strong."	didn't – din don't – don
Addition of schwa vowel /ə/ before /s/ or omission of /s/ in initial consonant clusters In Spanish, words cannot start with an /s/ cluster, but in English, they can.	study – estudy spoon – poon

Patterns of Native Language Influence:	Example:
Short English vowels that do not occur in Spanish may be substituted with a long vowel equivalent	witch – weetch sit- seat
Stops in word-initial position are unaspirated	pig – big

Difference or Disorder?

CONTRASTIVE ANALYSIS FOR SPEECH

Venn Contrast: Spanish & English Consonant Phonemes

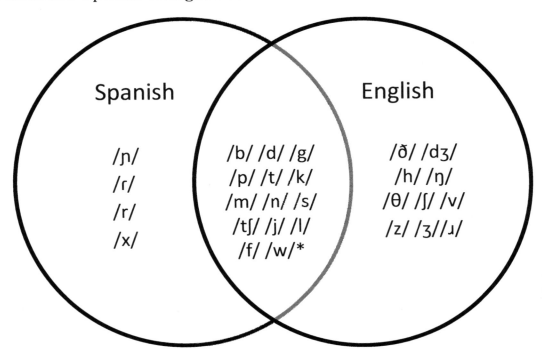

Venn Contrast: Spanish & English Vowel Phonemes

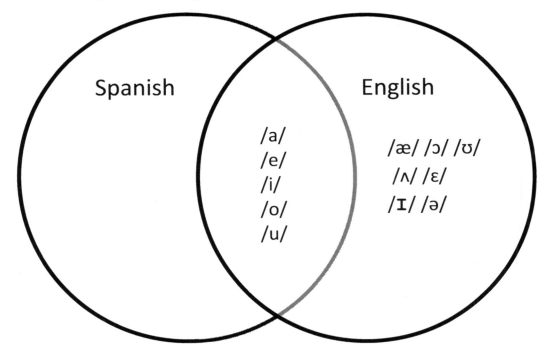

(Acevedo, 1993; Goldstein, 2007; Jimenez, 1987).

*/w/ is produced as a bilabial in English and as a labiovelar in Spanish.

DEVELOPMENTAL NORMS FOR LANGUAGE

Birth to 5 months

Reacts to loud noises	Birth to 3 months
Vocalizes discomfort, pleasure	4-6 months
Moves eyes toward direction of sound	4-5 months

6 to 12 months

Understands "no"	6-11 months
Babbles ("ma-ma-ma")	6-11 months
Uses gestures	7-12 months
Recognizes familiar objects when named	7-12 months
Says 1-2 words	12 months

1-2 years

Follows simple commands	12-15 months
Begins to respond to questions with gestures/pointing	12-17 months
Engages in symbolic play	18 months
Begins to combine 2 words ("more milk/ más leche")	1-2 years
Begins to make environmental noises (animal/car sounds)	1-2 years
Points to named items in book/picture	1-2 years

2-3 years

Responds to Yes/No questions	2-3 years
Combines 2-3 words to comment, inquire	2-3 year
Uses the present progressive verb form	2-3 years
Begins to use the plural form	2-3 years
Variety of consonants used in speech increases (t, d, k, g)	2-3 years
Speech is understood by familiar listeners most of the time	2-3 years
Uses regular past tense/simple preterit	2-3 years
Uses indefinite and definite articles	2-3 years
Follows 2-step directives	2-3 years
Article gender established	3 years

80

Difference or Disorder?

3-4 years

Engages in episodic play	3 years
Uses possessives	3-4 years
Uses irregular past tense (imperfect and preterit)	3-4 years
Uses negatives	3-4 years
Answer simple WH-?s	3-4 years
Generally speaks easily without effort in initiating sounds	3-4 years
Speech is generally understood by all	3-4 years
Begins to describe the use of objects	3-4 years
Shares personal experiences (school, friend's house)-short personal narratives	3-4 years
Combines 4+ words	3-4 years

4-5 years

Tells a story related to a topic	4-5 years
Produces most consonant sounds present in language	4-5 years
Uses the same grammar as family/home environment	4-5 years
Follows 3-step directions	4-5 years
Uses adjectives and descriptors in sentences	4-5 years

6-7 years

Narratives have a central point, climax, and resolution	5-7 years
Mastery of most consonants	6-7 years
Tells and re-tells stories in a logical order using complete sentences	6-7 years

7-9 years

Uses more complex sentence structures	7-8 years
Can clarify and explain ideas when not understood	7-8 years
Understands that words have synonyms, and multiple meanings	7-9 years
Narratives have complete episodes, including a setting, reaction of characters, conflict, and resolution	7-9 years

Expressive Vocabulary Development

2-5 words	12 months
4-6 words	15 months
20-50 words	18 months
200-300 words	24 months
~1000 words	36 months

(Prath, et al., 2012)

SPECIAL NOTE: VOCABULARY

The vocabulary choices of Spanish-English bilinguals acquiring the English language can provide insight about whether a student demonstrates a language difference or disorder. When bilingual children with typical development do not have the precise word for what they want to say, they often use words that are close in meaning to the target (e.g., "turtle" for "frog"). In contrast, bilingual children with language impairment often use nonspecific vocabulary ("this," "thing") more often than their typically developing peers (Kester, 2004). See the chart below for examples.

Target word	Semantically-related substitution	Nonspecific substitution
deer	moose	thing
frog	turtle	that

82

Difference or Disorder?

CONTRASTIVE ANALYSIS FOR LANGUAGE: MORPHOSYNTAX

Note: Sentences marked with an asterisk (*) are awkward or not grammatical.

Feature	Spanish	English	Examples of Errors
Word order	Flexible	Strict Subject-Verb-Object order	The ball he threw.*/ He threw the ball.
Possessives	noun+of+person	's	The car of my mom is blue*/ My mom's car is blue.
Adjectives	Adjective follows noun	Adjective precedes noun	The ball big bounced.*/ The big ball bounced.
Present tense verb inflection	5-6 forms, determined by subject: *Yo como* *Tú comes* *Él/Ella/Ud. come* *Nosotros comemos* *Vosotros coméis* *Ellos comen*	2 forms: I eat You eat He eats We eat You all eat They eat	She talk to me.* / She talks to me.
Use of subject pronouns	Pro-drop	Pronoun is always required	Looks for the frog* / He looks for the frog.
Regular past tense	5-6 forms, determined by subject	One form (-ed)	She walk to the store* / She walked to the store.
Double object pronoun	Can be used	Cannot be used	I saw him the man*/ I saw the man
Double negative	Can be used	Cannot be used	I don't want to do nothing*/ I don't want to do anything.
Question formation	Questions marked by inflection or question words	Questions marked by word order inversion, question words, or addition of *do*	You give me a sticker?*/ Will you give me a sticker? What you think?*/ What do you think? We can go?* / Can we go?
Multi-purpose verbs	Verbs with multiple meanings that do not always correspond to English	Verbs with multiple meanings that do not always correspond to Spanish	I have 4 years*/ I am four years old. Do you have hunger?*/ Are you hungry?

(Bedore, Peña, & Kester, 2007; Goldstein & Iglesias, 2006; Kester & Gorman, 2004; MacWhinney & Bates, 1989)

83

SPECIAL NOTE: PREPOSITIONS

Due to the frequency of preposition errors produced by Spanish speakers acquiring English, a few specific examples are provided below to assist in identifying second language influenced errors.

Spanish	English	Possible misuses of prepositions in English
En (in/on)	In/on	Put the food **in** the plate.*
		Put the food **on** the bowl.*
Pensar en/pensar de (think in/think of)	To think about or think of	I **think on** him everyday.*
		You can do it if you **think of** it.*
Enojarse con (to get mad with)	To get mad at	She **get mad with** me.*
Soñar con (to dream with)	To dream of	I **dreamt with you** last night*
Decidir de (to decide of)	To decide on	Have you **decided of** what you want?*
Casarse con (to marry with)	To marry or be married to	Is he **married with** her?*
Estar enamorado de (to be in love of)	To be in love with	Is he **in love of** her?*
Consistir en (to consist in)	To consist of	What does your plan consist **in**?*
Buscar (to look/search)	To look for	I'm **looking** my toy.*
Depender de (to depend of)	To depend on	It depends **of** what you want.*

Note: Sentences marked with an asterisk (*) are awkward or not grammatical.
Source: Kester & Gorman (2004).

HOME CORNER

As a bilingual speech language pathologist, I am grateful for my upbringing in a South Texas border town with a balanced blend of Mexican and American cultures. However, as a child I did not understand the value of knowing and understanding two cultures. Growing up, it was considered typical to speak English or Spanish depending on the situation or person. In more formal settings, such as school, I spoke only in English; however, with my family or in the community I was able to speak whichever language I felt was appropriate.

Difference or Disorder?

I remember having conversations with friends in both languages. At the time not knowing the term for what we were doing, code-switching, but, in our case it was not because of a lack of vocabulary in one language or the other. We did it to emphasize certain words or for humor. And to us, it was just...normal.

I took being bilingual for granted, always assuming that it would not be useful in my career, as the language of my formal education was in English. It was not until I moved away for college that I realized that being bilingual was needed in places that did not have such a seamless blend of cultures. It opened my eyes to the fact that I could help people, children and parents, who spoke Spanish like me. I became proud of my culture, instead of taking it for granted. When I assess bilingual children or have therapy sessions in Spanish, I can use the knowledge of my upbringing AND my formal education to make judgments and decisions regarding language differences and disorders.

Patricia Villarreal, Bilingual Speech-Language Pathologist

REFERENCES

Acevedo, M. (1993). Development of Spanish consonants in pre-school children. *Journal of Communication Disorders, 15*, 9–15.

Bedore, L. M., Peña, E. D., & Stubbe Kester, E. (2007). Cross language performance on semantic tasks: Lessons from a test development project. Manuscript in preparation.

Fabiano-Smith, L. & Goldstein, B. (2010). Phonological acquisition in bilingual Spanish-English speaking children. *Journal of Speech, Language, and Hearing Research, 53*. 1-19.

Goldstein, B., and Iglesias, A. (2006). Issues of cultural and linguistic diversity. In R. Paul and P. Cascella (Eds.). Introduction to clinical methods in communication disorders (2nd ed., pp. 261-280). Baltimore: Paul H. Brookes.

Goldman, R. (2000). Fristoe M. *Goldman-Fristoe Test of Articulation, 2*.

Jimenez, B. C. (1987). Acquisition of Spanish consonants in children aged 3-5 years, 7 months. *Language, Speech, and Hearing Services in Schools, 18*, 357–363.

Kester, E. S. & Gorman, B. K. (2004). Typical semantics and syntax in the English language learner. Austin: Bilinguistics.

MacWhinney, B. (1997). Second language acquisition and the competition model. In A.M.B. de Groot and J. F. Kroll (Eds.)*Tutorials in bilingualism: Psycholinguistic perspectives*. Mayway, NJ: Lawrence Erlbaum.

MacWhinney, B. & Bates, E. (Eds.) (1989). *The crosslinguistic study of sentence processing*. New York: Cambridge University Press.

Prath, S., Alvarez, A., Sanchez, K. A., Kester, E. S., Wirka, M. E., & Lebel, K. (2012). SMILE for Young Children. Austin, TX: Bilinguistics.

U. S. Census Bureau (2010). 2010 Census Data. Retrieved from http://www.census.gov/2010census/data/

Chapter 14
Vietnamese

"He that has a tongue in his head may find his way anywhere."

- Vietnamese Proverb

GENERAL INFORMATION

- **Number of speakers:** More than 1.5 million speakers of Vietnamese in the United States (U.S. Census, 2010)

- **Writing system:** The Vietnamese alphabet (quốc ngữ) in use today is a Latin alphabet with additional diacritics for tones, and certain letters.

- **Language Family:** Austro-Asiatic—Mon-Khmer—Viet-Muong

- **Official language in:** Vietnam and among approximately 3 million people residing in other locations around the world

PHONOLOGY AND PHONOTACTICS

Patterns of Native Language Influence:	Example:
Replacement of voiceless "th" (θ) with /t/ or /s/ in all positions	thumb – tum mouth – mous
Replacement of voiced "th" (ð) with /d/ or /z/ in all positions	they – dey the – dee
Replacement of /v/ with /b/ in all positions	very – bery
Replacement of /dʒ/ ("j") with /j/ ("y"), or vice-versa, in initial position	yellow – jello judge –yudge
Distortion of /ɹ/ in all positions, often resembling a trilled /r/ in initial position	/r/ can be distorted in a variety of ways
Omission or substitution of final consonants In Vietnamese, final consonants are voiceless stops (/t/, /k/, /p/ or nasals (/m/, /n/, /ŋ/); whereas, in English, many more consonants are allowed in this position.	Omissions wait – way eat – ee pass – pa Substitutions Off – op Bad – bat Tub – tup
Omission or distortion of consonant clusters Consonant clusters do not exist in Vietnamese. Vietnamese syllables are mostly consonant-vowel (CV). In English, there are a variety consonant clusters, such as /kst/ in "mixed" and /ŋz/ in "meetings."	didn't – din street – seet clean – cuh-lean

Difference or Disorder?

CONTRASTIVE ANALYSIS FOR SPEECH

Venn Contrast: Vietnamese & English Consonant Phonemes

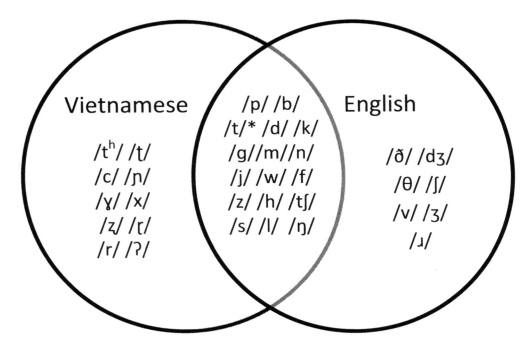

Venn Contrast: Vietnamese & English Vowel Phonemes

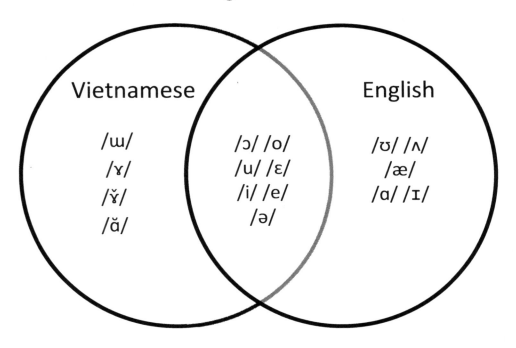

(Cheng, 1991; Hwa-Froelich, 2007; Hwa-Froelich, et al., 2002)

*/t/ is produced as a dentalized /t/ in Vietnamese.

CONTRASTIVE ANALYSIS FOR LANGUAGE: MORPHOSYNTAX

Note: Sentences marked with an asterisk (*) are not grammatical.

Feature	Vietnamese	English	Examples of Errors
Possessives	Noun + (prepositional phrase containing pronoun)	_____'s (singular nouns) _____s' (plural nouns)	I took the shoe of him.*/I took his shoe.
Adjectives	Adjective follows noun	Adjective precedes noun	The ball red is deflate.*/The red ball is deflated.
Plurality	Quantifiers precede the noun to mark plurality	Add an /s/ to the noun to mark plurality	We saw three bird in tree.*/We saw three birds in the tree.
Verb tense	Context and addition of words before or after the verb convey the tense	2 forms in present tense: I eat You eat He eats We eat You all eat They eat 1 form in regular past tense: -ed	I am eat.*/I am eating. She eat.*/She ate. Boy read.*/The boy will read.
Question formation	Question words are used with intonation in a subject-verb-object structure	Word order inversion or addition of the modal "do"	You want eat?*/Do you want to eat?
Negation	_No_ precedes the verbs When the copula is used, the negation phrase "không phải" is required	_Not_ comes before an auxiliary verb _Do_ comes before a main verb	I no want play.*/I don't want to play It no car me.*/That is not my car

HOME CORNER

I am a speech-language pathologist, and I am thrilled to be a part of such a meaningful profession. I will also acknowledge that a substantive part of what I bring to the table is my experience growing up bi-culturally. Growing up in a small, rural town in Texas, my school days, though impactful, felt alienating. I would put my best effort towards academic tasks. I assimilated to the task at hand, and (unintentionally) I, as a 7-seven-old, learned to discount my cultural background. There were times when I could think of a better

Difference or Disorder?

word, a Vietnamese word (!), to best describe a situation. I would bring the best, homemade lunches to school. Alas, due to snarky comments and my own sensitivities, I, too, brought bologna sandwiches and Doritos.

Over time (and with adult perspective), I embraced and validated what my parents, immigrants from Vietnam, provided and provided and provided. My culture, *my stories*, are made up of family, food, generational hardship, and personal successes. Now, each time I walk into a room to assist with an evaluation, interpret at a meeting, or conduct therapy, I feel like I am making my parents proud. I am not only providing a resource for my clients and students, but I am able to bring something that cannot be quantified on a standardized test or IEP paperwork. And, I am ever-so-grateful for the opportunity to acknowledge and validate these life matters.

Phuong Lien Palafox, Bilingual Speech-Language Pathologist

REFERENCES

Cheng, L. (1991). *Assessing Asian language performance: Guidelines for evaluating limited-English proficient students* (2nd ed.). Oceanside, CA: Academic Communication Associates.

Hwa-Froelich, D. (2007). Vietnamese speech acquisition. In McLeod, S. (Ed.), *The International Guide to Speech Acquisition* (pp. 580-591). Clifton Park, NY: Thompson Delmar Learning.

Hwa-Froelich, D., Hodson, B., & Edwards, H. (2002). Characteristics of Vietnamese phonology. *American Journal of Speech-Language Pathology, 11*, 264-273.

Kohnert, K. (2008). *Language disorders in bilingual children and adults.* San Diego, CA: Plural Publishing.

Nguyen, V. S., Carré, R., & Castelli, E. (2008). Production and perception of Vietnamese short vowels. In *Acoustical Society of America Meeting* (pp. 3509-3514). Paris.

Pham, G. and Kohnert, K. (2008). Vietnamese-English bilingual children assessment and intervention. Paper presented at American Speech Hearing Association National Convention in Chicago, IL, 2008.

Roseberry-McKibbin, C. (2008). Language differences commonly observed among Asian speakers from multicultural students with special language needs. Oceanside, CA: Academic Communication Associates. p.123-134.

Tang, G. (2007). Cross-linguistic analysis of Vietnamese and English with implications for Vietnamese language acquisition and maintenance in the United States. *Journal of Southeast Asian-American Education and Advancement, 2*, 1-33.

U. S. Census Bureau (2010). 2010 Census Data. Retrieved at http://www.census.gov/2010census/data/

Chapter 15
African-American English

GENERAL INFORMATION

African-American English is a dialect of American English. It is spoken by many, but not all African-Americans, as well as people of other races and ethnicities throughout the United States. Its usage may be influenced by a variety of factors such as age, education, and style. Linguistically, African-American English shares features of Southern American English dialect and many African creole dialects, and it is considered by some to be a creole. Its cultural relevance is well recognized in literature and music. While controversy exists about the use of this dialect, especially in educational settings, speech-language pathologists and educators are very likely to encounter it among their students.

African-American students have historically been over-represented in special education. African-American youth, ages 6 through 21, account for 14.8 percent of the general population, yet they account for 20.2 percent of the special education population (OSEP, 2000). This is an alarming percentage that moves us to ask why this is the case. Many of these children enter special education with a diagnosis of speech and/or language impairments. In order to accurately diagnose impairments, an understanding of dialectical influences on language is critical. Just as we consider the language differences of children whose first language is other than English, we should consider the language differences of children whose dialect is other than "standard." The research supports that "there is a marked increase in the use of African-American English (AAE) features between the ages of three and five" (Bland-Stewart, 2005), which coincides with most children's entry into the U.S. Education System. "Dialect shifting to Mainstream American English (MAE) appears to emerge between Kindergarten and 2nd grade" (Craig & Washington, 2004). The majority of students with speech and language impairments in the school setting are likely to be identified between the ages of three and nine, or between preschool and third grade.

In order to perform a non-biased, culturally appropriate evaluation of the speech and language skills of speakers of African-American English, there must be awareness of its differences from Standard American English in order to make a determination of dialectal difference versus disorder. A presentation of the different features will assist in conducting valid and non-biased assessments of speakers of this dialect.

DEVELOPMENTAL NORMS FOR SPEECH AND LANGUAGE

According to Bland-Stewart (2005), "Language development in African-American English-speaking children is similar to that of Standard American English-speaking children up to age 3 across content, form, and use. However, under 3 years of age it is difficult to distinguish between dialectal and developmental variations." Therefore, it is expected that early developmental milestones up to age 3 are similar for Standard American English-speaking children and African-American English-speaking children.

Difference or Disorder?

CONTRASTIVE ANALYSIS FOR SPEECH

There are numerous dialectal differences between African-American English (AAE) and Standard American English (SAE) in the areas of phonology, phonotactics, morphosyntax, and semantics. Examples of common differences can be seen below.

PHONOLOGY AND PHONOTACTICS

Frequent Dialectal Difference Patterns:	Example:
Replacement of voiced "th"(ð) with /d/ in the initial position	them – dem
Replacement of voiced "th" (ð) with /v/ in the medial position	brother – brover
Replacement of voiceless "th" (θ) with /f/ in medial and final positions	birthday – birfday south – souf
Omission of /ɹ/ after a vowel and in final position	fort – fought door – doe
Omission of /ɹ/ between a consonant and a back-rounded vowel	throw – thow
Omission of /l/ in combination with cluster simplification and final consonant deletion	told – toe tool – too
Devoicing or omission of final consonants, including "g" dropping (i.e., replacing /ŋ/ ("ng") with /n/)	cub – cup his – hiss looking – lookin man –maa
Reduction of final consonant clusters in singular nouns Pattern may not apply when final consonants are voiced + voiceless (e.g., 'nt' in sent).	test – tes hand – han
Reduction of final consonant clusters in plural nouns	tests – tesses wasps – wasses
Metathesis (sound reversal) within consonant clusters, with or without consonant reduplication	ask – axe escape – ekscape
Replacement of consonant cluster "str" with "skr"	street – skreet
Omission of unstressed syllables in multisyllabic words	became – came
Addition of syllables	forests – forestses
Reduction of certain diphthongs to monophthongs, long vowels to short vowels (especially before /l/ and /r/), and high vowels to low vowels (especially before nasals) This is also a feature of many Southern U.S. dialects.	boil – ball our – are feel – fill thing – thang pen – pin

(Craig, Thompson, Washington, & Potter, 2003; Craig, Kolenic, & Hensel, 2013; Packer, 2001)

SPECIAL NOTE: VOCABULARY

African-American English shares the majority of its vocabulary with other English dialects, especially Southern United States English, although some lexical variations do exist. These include both unique words and words whose meanings differ from their usage in Standard American English (e.g., "threads" meaning clothes). Many words and phrases that originated in African-American English have become part of Standard American English, such as "chill out" and "funky."

CONTRASTIVE ANALYSIS FOR LANGUAGE: MORPHOSYNTAX

Note: Sentences in italics are grammatical dialectical variations.

Feature	AAE	SAE	Examples
Present tense verb "to be"	Can be used, omitted, or substituted as determined by context and contractibility	Must always be included	*He a boy.* He is a boy. *He eatin'.* / He is eating. *The coffee bees cold.*/ The coffee is cold. *There go a bus.*/ There is a bus.
Past tense verb "to be"	Uses the same form (i.e., "was") with all persons and numbers	Uses "was" for 1st and 3rd person singular and "were" for all other persons and numbers	*You was going to go.*/You were going to go. *We was going to go.*/We were going to go.
Habitual/ continuative state	Allows for inflection of the verb "to be"	Expressed through adverbs and inflected forms of the verb "to be"	*He be waiting all day.*/ He waits all day. *She been buying me clothes.*/ She has been buying me clothes (for a long time).

Difference or Disorder?

Feature	AAE	SAE	Examples
Regular past tense marker: –ed	Omitted and optional tenses/phases permitted	Required in regular verbs	*He start crying an hour ago./* He started crying an hour ago. *She been done./* She finished work (a long time ago). *They been had that dog./* They had the dog (for years).
Irregular past tense verbs	Past participle is substituted	Past tense verb is used	*She seen him./* She saw him. *He knowed it./* He knew it.
Modals	Uses double modals for "might," "could," "should"	Uses single modals	*I might could play./* I might be able to play.
Present and past perfect verb forms	"Been" or "done" are used to show past action that has been completed recently or to emphasize that it was completed a long time ago	Uses "have, has, had" plus "been"	*I been there before./* I have been there before. *I been finished./* I have finished./ *He been gone./* He's been gone for a long time.
Future tense verbs	"Will" is not used and "fixing to" (minus the auxiliary verb) is substituted for "is going to"	"Will" is inserted before "be" or the auxiliary + -ing is used	*They be here soon./* They will be here soon. *He finna* (also written fixina, fixna, fitna, finta, fittin) *go./* He is going to go.
Negation	Use of multiple negatives and the word *ain't* is permitted	Single negatives and the contractions *isn't, aren't, hasn't, don't, haven't*	*Nobody don't never agree with me./* No one ever agrees with me. *I ain't goin./* I'm not going.

Feature	AAE	SAE	Examples
Third person singular –s	Omitted or used with the 1st person and may mark both a main verb and an infinitive in the same sentence	Added to the verb	*The boy want to run./* The boy wants to run. *I does./* I do. *She wants to eats it./* She wants to eat it.
Plural –s	Is omitted to reduce redundancy with nouns of measure (i.e., numbers)	Is used to mark plurals	*He have fifty cent./* He has fifty cents. *Here two shoe./* Here are two shoes.
Irregular plurals	Plural –s is added	Forms are few and varied	*They have three childs./* They have three children.
Possessive –s	Is absent or is used when possession is already marked	The 's is used to mark possession	*That John ball./* That is John's ball. *The car is mine's./* The car is mine.
Pronouns	Substitutions of subject, object and possessive pronouns are common.	Forms do not vary	*I need them books./* I need those books. *That they laundry./* That is their laundry.
Article "an"	Is substituted with "a" before nouns beginning with a vowel	Is used before nouns beginning with a vowel	*I want a apple./* I want an apple.
Prepositions	Are distributed differently or are omitted	Must be included	*Where my car at?/* Where's my car? *We got out here./* We got out of here.

Difference or Disorder?

Feature	AAE	SAE	Examples
Questions	Invert the verb in indirect questions	Use different forms for direct and indirect questions	*What it is?/* What is it?
Conditional	Use "do" in place of "if," omit "if" from embedded questions	Use conditional "if"	*I wonder did she go./* I wonder if she went. *They asked could I go./* They asked if I could go.
Comparative and superlative	Uses root word with –er in comparative form and adds –est to superlative form	Uses –er with comparative and –est with superlative	*This car gooder./* This car is better. *He is the bestest./* He is the best.

Bland-Stewart, 2005; Craig & Grogger, 2012; Craig, Kolenic, & Hensel, 2013; Green & Stockman, 2003; Packer, M. 2001; Wikipedia, 2013; Wood & Lyngaas, 1995)

HOME CORNER

I am a speech-language pathologist who grew up as a bi-dialectal speaker. My first dialect is African-American English and my second dialect is Standard American English. I did not begin speaking Standard American English until my adolescent years. During these years, I found my passion for language. At that time I did not understand the complexities of being able to speak both African-American English and Standard American English. Even now I am amazed at how beautiful, yet complicated, it is to be bi-dialectal in America.

I recall growing up in an African-American community. There was always a love for language; this was demonstrated in music, poetry, and everyday lingo. It was a way to connect with my peers and family members, express my thoughts, and gain a sense of belonging. Occasionally, I would see an individual who spoke Standard American English and my peers would state "they were talking funny." Eventually this person felt a sense of loneliness and was never openly received in the community. I always knew my first dialect was my connection with my community and I could never lose it in order to make others in the mainstream population happy.

On the other hand, in school I was expected to speak Standard American English. I was presented with books and tests that were written and normalized on Standard American English speakers and I was expected to be successful. However, most teachers did not know how to address the needs of students who spoke African-American English in their lessons. There were teachers who had a negative view about African-American English, thus they viewed the speaker of African-American English as intellectually deficient. There were other teachers who did not feel comfortable speaking to the parents of African-American English speakers to design a plan to assist the learner who speaks African-American English in the schools. As a speech-language pathologist, I still see both of these situations occurring in the school setting. Luckily, I had awesome parents who served as my greatest advocates. When I began to have trouble in school, they believed in me and communicated the importance of code-switching. My parents did not force me to speak Standard American English in elementary or middle school. My parents, grandparents, and great-grandparents always reminded me of how beautiful African-American English was. My mentors reminded me of how my ancestors came to America and did not have the ability to communicate with each other or in the American society. However, they were able to form a language, a dialect of their own that allowed them to experience the gift of communication. I always felt a sense of pride when I heard how African-American English was formed. But reality was setting in; I was in high school preparing for college. Most of the tests utilized to determine my future were normalized on Standard American English speakers. I knew that when I received my scores, they would not take into account my background. Thus, I had to learn the importance of being proud of who I was, and knowing the difference of who I

Difference or Disorder?

could be if I had the ability to code-switch. With the help of countless tutors and amazing

mentors (including my parents, who are bi-dialectal), I was able to join a field where I could

be an advocate for culturally and linguistically diverse speakers. I am now able to utilize my

experiences as a bi-dialectal speaker to advocate for others and teach my colleagues about

language differences and language disorders.

Brittney Donielle Goodman M.S., CCC-SLP, Speech-Language Pathologist

REFERENCES

Bland-Stewart, L. (2005). Difference or deficit in speakers of African American English?: What Every Clinician Should Know . . . and Do. United States: The ASHA Leader.

Craig, H., Thompson, C., Washington, J., & Potter, S. (2003). Phonological features of child African American English. *Journal of Speech, Language, and Hearing Reseach, 46,* 623-635.

Craig, H. K., & Washington, J. A. (2004). Grade-related changes in the production of African American English. *Journal of Speech, Language, and Hearing Research, 47*(2), 450-463.

Craig, H., & Grogger, J. (2012). Influences of social and style variables on adult usage of African American English features. *Journal of Speech, Language, and Hearing Research, 55,* 1274-1288.

Craig, H., Kolenic, G., Hensel, S. (2013). African American English speaking students: A longitudinal examination of style shifting from kindergarten through second grade. *Journal of Speech, Language, and Hearing Research, 57,* 143-157.

Green, L. & Stockman, I. (2003). *Alternate responses to the word structure subtest items for speakers of African American English.* San Antonio, TX: Pearson.

OSEP (2000). Twenty-Second Annual Report to Congress on the Implementation of the Individuals with Disabilities Education Act. Retrieved from http://www2.ed.gov/about/reports/annual/osep/2000/index.html

Packer, M. (2001). Black English [Class handout]. Pittsburgh, PA: Duquesne University.

Wikipedia. (2013). African American vernacular English. Retrieved from <http://en.wikipedia.org/wiki/African_American_Vernacular_English>, accessed Nov. 5, 2013.

Wood, M. and Lyngaas, K. (1995). Grammatical contrasts between Black English and Standard American English. Madison, WI: Madison Metropolitan School District.

Chapter 16
Quick Tips for Assessing in *Any* Language

More than 6,500 languages are spoken on this planet, and there is a way to positively approach assessments of clients and students from culturally and linguistically diverse backgrounds. This text is designed to simplify the process for a handful of languages, but you can follow these steps to implement this process for other languages. Here's how:

1. Research the child's native language. Type the language into any search engine and, presto! There is a lot of information out there. How do we get what we need? We approach it like a news reporter. We find a source, and then look for at least one other source to verify the information. There is a high degree of variation in language development, which is often seen in the developmental norms that are available.

2. If you are assessing articulation, look at the sounds that exist in that particular language. Typically, you can find a chart with the sounds used in that language.

Look at the chart. Are there sounds that exist in English that do **not** exist in the student's native language? If so, these would **not** be sounds that we would expect in

Phonology [edit]

Main article: Gujarati phonology

				Consonants					
		Bilabial	Labio-dental	Dental/Alveolar	Retroflex	Post-alv./Palatal	Velar	Glottal
Nasal		m		n	ɳ			
Plosive		p b / pʰ bʱ		t̪ d̪ / t̪ʰ d̪ʱ	ʈ ɖ / ʈʰ ɖʱ		k g / kʰ gʱ	
Affricate						t͡ʃ d͡ʒ / t͡ʃʰ d͡ʒʱ		
Fricative				s		ʃ		ɦ
Tap or Flap				ɾ				
Approximant		ʋ		l	ɭ	j		

Vowels			
	Front	Central	Back
Close	i		u
Mid	e		o
	ɛ	ə	ɔ
Open		ɑ	

English, nor good sounds to address in therapy. Tackle the sounds that exist in <u>both</u> languages if they are difficult for your student.

3. If you are assessing language concepts, look at the syntactic features for that particular language. Again, you will likely be able to find a chart or information on specific features of the language. For example:

> # Punjabi has a canonical word order of SOV (subject–object–verb). It has postpositions rather than prepositions.

If you see the previous statement, it would tell you that errors regarding word order when speaking English may be influenced by one's native language of Punjabi. There may also be prepositional errors, and that would be acceptable since prepositions are not used in Punjabi.

Obviously, the quick tips above are a simplification of what can be a very lengthy process. Gathering the right speech and language information can take a while. Luckily, we have completed this process for you by compiling the information you need from a variety

104

Difference or Disorder?

of sources. The Bilinguistics team is continually adding new languages and new information

to our resources. If there is a language you need information about, contact us. You can

find our contact information on our website at www.bilinguistics.com.

105

Appendix A: IPA Chart

THE INTERNATIONAL PHONETIC ALPHABET (revised to 2005)

CONSONANTS (PULMONIC)

© 2005 IPA

	Bilabial	Labiodental	Dental	Alveolar	Postalveolar	Retroflex	Palatal	Velar	Uvular	Pharyngeal	Glottal
Plosive	p b			t d		ʈ ɖ	c ɟ	k g	q ɢ		ʔ
Nasal	m	ɱ		n		ɳ	ɲ	ŋ	N		
Trill	ʙ			r					R		
Tap or Flap		ⱱ		ɾ		ɽ					
Fricative	ɸ β	f v	θ ð	s z	ʃ ʒ	ʂ ʐ	ç ʝ	x ɣ	χ ʁ	ħ ʕ	h ɦ
Lateral fricative				ɬ ɮ							
Approximant		ʋ		ɹ		ɻ	j	ɰ			
Lateral approximant				l		ɭ	ʎ	L			

Where symbols appear in pairs, the one to the right represents a voiced consonant. Shaded areas denote articulations judged impossible.

CONSONANTS (NON-PULMONIC)

Clicks	Voiced implosives	Ejectives
ʘ Bilabial	ɓ Bilabial	ʼ Examples:
ǀ Dental	ɗ Dental/alveolar	pʼ Bilabial
ǃ (Post)alveolar	ʄ Palatal	tʼ Dental/alveolar
ǂ Palatoalveolar	ɠ Velar	kʼ Velar
ǁ Alveolar lateral	ʛ Uvular	sʼ Alveolar fricative

OTHER SYMBOLS

- ʍ Voiceless labial-velar fricative
- w Voiced labial-velar approximant
- ɥ Voiced labial-palatal approximant
- ʜ Voiceless epiglottal fricative
- ʢ Voiced epiglottal fricative
- ʡ Epiglottal plosive
- ɕ ʑ Alveolo-palatal fricatives
- ɺ Voiced alveolar lateral flap
- ɧ Simultaneous ʃ and x

Affricates and double articulations can be represented by two symbols joined by a tie bar if necessary. k͡p t͡s

VOWELS

Where symbols appear in pairs, the one to the right represents a rounded vowel.

SUPRASEGMENTALS

- ˈ Primary stress
- ˌ Secondary stress   ˌfoʊnəˈtɪʃən
- ː Long   eː
- ˑ Half-long   eˑ
- ̆ Extra-short   ĕ
- | Minor (foot) group
- ‖ Major (intonation) group
- . Syllable break   ɹi.ækt
- ‿ Linking (absence of a break)

TONES AND WORD ACCENTS

LEVEL		CONTOUR	
e̋ or ˥	Extra high	ě or ˩˥	Rising
é ˦	High	ê ˥˩	Falling
ē ˧	Mid	e᷄ ˦˥	High rising
è ˨	Low	e᷅ ˩˨	Low rising
ȅ ˩	Extra low	e᷈ ˧˦˧	Rising-falling
↓	Downstep	↗	Global rise
↑	Upstep	↘	Global fall

DIACRITICS
Diacritics may be placed above a symbol with a descender, e.g. ŋ̊

Voiceless	n̥ d̥	Breathy voiced	b̤ a̤	Dental	t̪ d̪
Voiced	s̬ t̬	Creaky voiced	b̰ a̰	Apical	t̺ d̺
Aspirated	tʰ dʰ	Linguolabial	t̼ d̼	Laminal	t̻ d̻
More rounded	ɔ̹	Labialized	tʷ dʷ	Nasalized	ẽ
Less rounded	ɔ̜	Palatalized	tʲ dʲ	Nasal release	dⁿ
Advanced	u̟	Velarized	tˠ dˠ	Lateral release	dˡ
Retracted	e̠	Pharyngealized	tˤ dˤ	No audible release	d̚
Centralized	ë	Velarized or pharyngealized	ɫ		
Mid-centralized	e̽	Raised	e̝ (ɹ̝ = voiced alveolar fricative)		
Syllabic	n̩	Lowered	e̞ (β̞ = voiced bilabial approximant)		
Non-syllabic	e̯	Advanced Tongue Root	e̘		
Rhoticity	ɚ a˞	Retracted Tongue Root	e̙		

Appendix B: English Developmental Charts

DEVELOPMENTAL NORMS FOR SPEECH

Age	Sounds
3	/m, n, p, b, w, h/
3.5	/k, d, f/
4	/g, t/
5	/ y, blends/
5.5	/v/
6	/l/
7	/ʧ, ʃ, j, ð, ʤ/
8	/ŋ, ɹ, s, z, θ, ʒ /

DEVELOPMENTAL NORMS FOR PHONOLOGICAL PROCESSES

Age of Suppression	Phonological process
3	Pre-vocalic voicing, Word-final consonant devoicing
4	Final consonant deletion, Fronting, Consonant harmony, Weak syllable deletion, Cluster reduction
5	Stopping, Gliding
7	Vocalization

DEVELOPMENTAL NORMS FOR LANGUAGE

Birth to 5 months	
Reacts to loud noises	Birth to 3 months
Vocalizes discomfort, pleasure	4-6 months
Moves eyes toward direction of sound	4-5 months

6 to 12 months	
Understands "no"	6-11 months
Babbles ("ma-ma-ma")	6-11 months
Uses gestures	7-12 months
Recognizes familiar objects when named	7-12 months
Says 1-2 words	12 months

1-2 years

Follows simple commands	12-15 months
Begins to respond to questions with gestures/pointing	12-17 months
Engages in symbolic play	18 months
Begins to combine 2 words ("more milk")	1-2 years
Begins to make environmental noises (animal/car sounds)	1-2 years
Points to named items in book/picture	1-2 years

2-3 years

Responds to Yes/No questions	2-3 years
Combines 2-3 words to comment, inquire	2-3 year
Uses the present progressive verb form	2-3 years
Begins to use the plural form	2-3 years
Variety of consonants used in speech increases (t, d, k, g)	2-3 years
Speech is understood by familiar listeners most of the time	2-3 years
Uses regular past tense/simple preterit	2-3 years
Uses indefinite and definite articles	2-3 years
Follows 2-step directives	2-3 years
Article gender established	3 years

3-4 years

Engages in episodic play	3 years
Uses possessives	3-4 years
Uses Irregular past tense/Imperfect Preterit	3-4 years
Uses negatives	3-4 years
Answers simple Wh- questions	3-4 years
Generally speaks easily without effort in initiating sounds	3-4 years
Shares personal experiences and short narratives	3-4 years
Combines 4+ words	3-4 years

108

Difference or Disorder?

4-5 years

Tells a story related to a topic	4-5 years
Produces most consonant sounds present in language	4-5 years
Uses the same grammar as family/home environment	4-5 years
Follows 3-step directions	4-5 years
Uses adjectives and descriptors in sentences	4-5 years

6-7 years

Tells and re-tells stories in a logical order using complete sentences	6-7 years

7-8 years

Uses more complex sentence structures	7-8 years
When not understood, can clarify and explain ideas	7-8 years

(Prath, et al., 2012)

REFERENCES

Bowen, C. (1998). Developmental phonological disorders. A practical guide for   families and teachers. Melbourne: ACER Press.

N.A. (2003). Speech & Articulation Development Chart. Retrieved May 5, 2014, from Talking Child: http://talkingchild.com/speechchart.aspx.

Grunwell, P. (1997). Natural phonology. In M. Ball & R. Kent (Eds.), The new phonologies: Developments in clinical linguistics. San Deigo, CA: Singular Publishing Group, Inc.

Howard, M. R., & Hulit, L. M. (2001). Born to Talk: An Introduction to Speech and Language Development.

Paul, R. (2007). Language disorders from infancy through adolescence: Assessment & intervention. Elsevier Health Sciences.

Prath, S., Alvarez, A., Sanchez, K. A., Kester, E. S., Wirka, M. E., & Lebel, K. (2012). SMILE for Young Children. Austin, TX: Bilinguistics.

Rosetti, L. (2006). The Infant-Toddler Language Scale. Linguisystems, East Moline, IL: Linguisystems.

Shriberg, L. D. (1993). Four new speech and prosody-voice measures for genetics research and other studies in developmental phonological disorders. Journal of Speech, Language, and Hearing Research, 36(1), 105-140.

Wein. H. (Ed.) (2007) Is baby babbling on schedule? Milestones in speech and   language. National Institutes of Health. Accessed via http://newsinhealth.nih.gov/pdf/NIHNiH%20September07.pdf on 1 May 2014.

Zimmerman, I. L., Steiner, V. G., & Pond, R. E. (2002). Preschool Language Scale, Fourth Edition. Pearson: San Antonio.

Made in the USA
Lexington, KY
07 March 2018